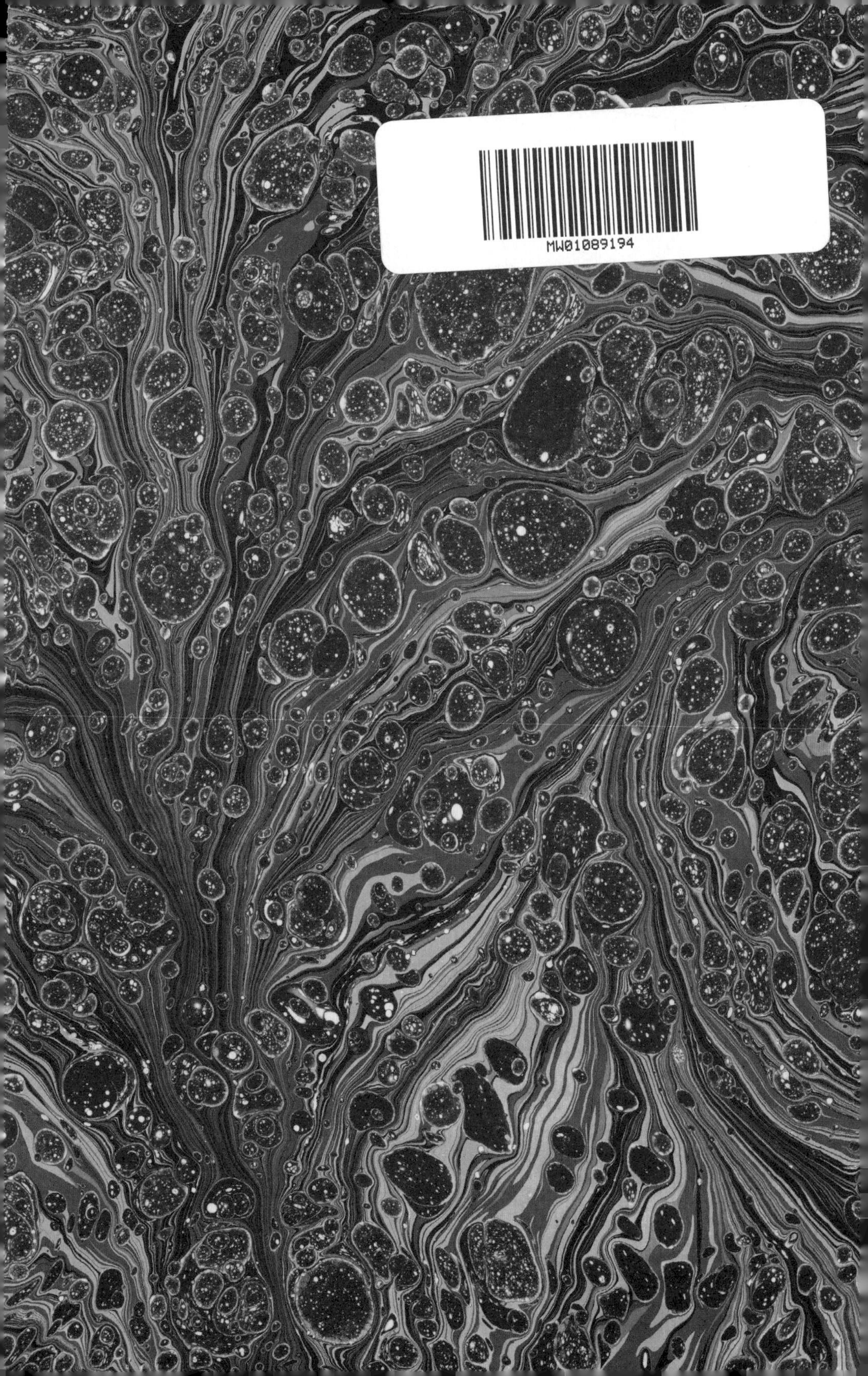
MW01089194

THE CLAY PIGEONS

To Mike –
a trusted friend,
always.

Helene
12/8/11

Lt. Robert Charles Sage, 8th Air Force, 306th Heavy Bombardment Group, 367th Bomb Squadron (Clay Pigeons).

THE CLAY PIGEONS

A B-17 Pilot's Story of World War II

E. Helene Sage

Schiffer Military History
Atglen, PA

Dedication

To my father, Robert Charles Sage (RCS), a member of the Eighth Air Force and "The Greatest Generation"

Book Design by Ian Robertson.

Library of Congress Control Number: 2011936124

Printed in China.
ISBN: 978-0-7643-3951-6

We are interested in hearing from authors with book ideas on related topics.

Published by Schiffer Publishing Ltd.
4880 Lower Valley Road
Atglen, PA 19310
Phone: (610) 593-1777
FAX: (610) 593-2002
E-mail: Info@schifferbooks.com.
Visit our web site at: www.schifferbooks.com
Please write for a free catalog.
This book may be purchased from the publisher.
Please include $5.00 postage.
Try your bookstore first.

In Europe, Schiffer books are distributed by:
Bushwood Books
6 Marksbury Avenue
Kew Gardens
Surrey TW9 4JF, England
Phone: 44 (0) 20 8392-8585
FAX: 44 (0) 20 8392-9876
E-mail: Info@bushwoodbooks.co.uk.
Visit our website at: www.bushwoodbooks.co.uk

Contents

Acknowledgments

My debt to the men and women who served in World War II as part of the Allied Cause is inestimable.

I thank Schiffer Publishing, Ltd., for their enthusiasm and assistance in the preparation of this book, and especially Pete Schiffer and Ian Robertson. Eileen Neligan prepared the manuscript with her expertise and enthusiasm that I never cease to appreciate.

My brother, Robert Charles Sage, Jr., was instrumental in the assembly of our father's medals, photographs, and other information pertaining to his service in World War II for submission to the Mighty Eighth Air Force Museum in Savannah, Georgia. My uncle, Harry Russell Sage, generously provided family background and information from the early years through World War II. Dianne S. James unselfishly shared documentation and photographs of Lt. Sage from the War years. I thank Karen Sage for the photography of RCS's flight jacket that appears on the cover of this book.

I am indebted to Vivian Rogers-Price, Ph.D., Director, Roger A. Freeman Eighth Air Force Research Center, for her advice and guidance toward important literature and databases pertaining to World War II and the "Mighty Eighth." Jean Prescott (librarian, Mighty Eighth Air Force Museum) retrieved data and helped with resources needed for the book.

Little would have been possible without the support of my husband, Paul Bornstein, M.D., himself a survivor of the Second World War, who provides wise counsel and invaluable perspective.

Introduction

Shortly after its publication, my copy of *The Greatest Generation* by Tom Brokaw (Brokaw, 1998) was given to me by my father, Robert Charles Sage, First Lieutenant, Army Air Corps (ret.), with the following inscription: "For your enjoyment and understanding of our greatest generation! Dad." And I did read it, all of it, and came away with a profound feeling of both indebtedness and regret—too many stories were left untold, and too much history, personal and national, was left unrecorded. My father was a member of the Eighth Air Force, the Clay Pigeons (367th Bomb Squadron [B.S.], 306th Heavy Bombardment Group [B.G.]), stationed in Thurleigh, Bedfordshire, England. He was pilot or co-pilot of B-17 bombers and flew 29 missions in the European Theater, from May 8 to August 24, 1944. A member of the Regular Army from February 7, 1943, to December 4, 1943, he was honorably discharged to accept a commission in the Army Air Corps on December 5, 1943, and was discharged in October 1945, having received the Distinguished Flying Cross, European-African-Middle Eastern Campaign Medal, and four Air Medals (3 Oak Leaf clusters)(Ehli, 2002). Upon his death in 2002, I received his Pilot Flight Record and Log Book (1943), a series of military photographs, and a personal diary, including a detailed list of missions flown, with entries from April 12 to September 7, 1944. Neither my brother nor I had been aware of the existence of this diary—and little information had been forthcoming during our childhood about my father's experiences in World War II. It would not be difficult to understand that such memories were suppressed or, at best, pushed aside as one reentered civilian life and proceeded with an allegedly "normal" routine. But it could never have been entirely normal—the diary attests to the seven months of trial that most of us would otherwise be unable to imagine. Yet, it is not an emotional "tell-all" documentary. The diary presents facts, dates, locations, names of crewmen and fellow officers, visits to London and nearby villages, living conditions, and most importantly, details of missions, ground school, and B-17s (the Flying Fortresses), all of historical relevance.

Remarkable entries include those from D-Day:

June 6. "D-Day" Clay Pidgeon. "Up at 23:45. Didn't even get to sleep. Went on mission to Anselles-Sur-Mer, on French Coast. Bombed gun emplacements, troops, etc. Carried 38-100 lbs. demolition bombs. 1700 gals. fuel. Bombed from 16,000'. Invasion began at 07:25. Zero hour was 07:30. Our group put up 42 ships in first wave, and 12 in second. 1,350 heavy bombers were in the first wave, & 550 in second. 11,000 planes will be over coast during day. Some Blitz. We bombed PFF- "Gee Box." Mission last 4-1/2 hours. We are alerted again. Up at 15:00. Went to Thury-Harcourt, Coast of France. Bombed in front of our landing troops. Bombed an important road junction. Dropped 12- 500 lbs. bombs. Just group leader (PFF) and us went in alone. Rest of formation didn't find us. Lots of clouds. Good ringside seat up there. Ships and boats of all kinds. Men on beach. Fire and hell all over coast. Bombed from 17,000'. Mission 4-1/2 hours. Landed 22:45. Plenty tired.

And the christening of the "Rose of York" by Princess Elizabeth:

July 6. Clay Pidgeons. "Up at 08:00. Combat meeting, etc. Flew in formation over field as Royal Family and Doolittle were here at Princess's christening of the "Rose of York." Mac was co-pilot. Raster pilot. Raster received captain's bars today also. Went with Malsom's crew tonight to Red Cross Aeroclub for dinner. Very nice. Toast and butter with Carter and Shaw, and to bed. Malan was hit in forearm today by .50 cal. bullet. Over at Dittingdon now in hospital."

Several entries are notable for their descriptions of critical missions (Poland, Germany, Belgium, and France), as well as incredible details concerning the formations, bombs, and the pervading threat of anti-aircraft enemy flak. Clearly one of the most debilitating aspects of these missions was the lack of sleep experienced by the crews—over 50% of the entries in the diary refer to the need, lack of, or desire for rest and untroubled sleep:

May 8. Clay Pidgeon. "Up at 01:30 this morning. Briefed at 03:00. Went to Berlin. Took off at 06:15. Arrived target about 11:00. We dropped behind formation. Salvoed bombs to catch up. Poor engines. Not too much flak. No fighters. Carried 10- 500 lbs. Also chaff. Saw 3 ships collide and blow up immediately in front of us. Not too crazy about this stuff. Flak pretty accurate. Cloud cover-bombed by PFF. Letter from Dad here. Sleep-sleep-sleep. P.S. Our own fighter support was good. The three ships lost were from our squadron. Five from our group. Took 9 hrs. 40 min. -47 degrees. Nearly froze. No heater. Flak hole in right wing, outside #4 engine. Everybody OK. Flew over Amsterdam on return."

May 12. Clay Pidgeon. "Up at 01:40. Briefing 02:00. We went to Merseburg, Germany, and bombed the Leuna Oil Plant. Produces 600,000 gals. Synthetic aviation gasoline yearly. We blew the hell out of it. Huge fires & black columns of black smoke. We had old #729- open waist windows. Ristuccia and Dickhaus were both frost-bitten on the face. Not a flak hole. We flew #6 in high squadron. Tired—to bed…"

May 13. Clay Pidgeon. "Up at 05:00. Briefed at 06:00. Went on raid to bomb Stettin, in old Poland. Bombed PFF. An 11-hour haul. Flew over Denmark, and just south of Sweden. We flew #3 in lead sqdn. and lead groups, on Col. Raper's left wing. PFF ship. Very heavy flak. We had at least 30 holes in our plane. Flak was very accurate, also. One piece came in under windshield & hit steering column & up and out other side of cockpit. Another piece through side, inch behind my foot, down through floor. Plenty rough. #4, new ship, ditched. All men saved. Our ship #278, its first mission, full of holes. Rough one… To bed—exhausted."

May 23. Clay Pidgeon. "Up at 03:00. Went on raid to Saarbrucken, but we "aborted" about ½ hour before I.P. With Allen's crew. Crunican was along. #4 engine caught fire, turned back, engine wouldn't feather, fire went out. We let down to 10,000 ft. on top of cloud-deck, few minutes four beautiful P51's escorted us all the way home. Two P47's looked us over too. Three engines got us home O.K. We salvoed our bombs "safe" over France to lighten load. Flak picked us up on the way out. About ten holes. Chuck had his hand splintered with plexi-glass. Probably Purple Heart. Not seriously injured. I'm exhausted. Slept all afternoon. To bed again."

May 31. Clay Pidgeon. "Went to Airfield at Liege, Belgium. Made three runs over target. We salvoed our bombs on last run. I was with Malsom. Lost #4 engine on first run, hit #3 on second run. Feathered both engines and came home alone on two engines. Towering cumulus clouds-rime-ice. Piece flak size of a baseball came through floor under my left foot, and out my side under window. Expected to ditch but did not have to. Made R.A.F field on English coast. Landed at 12:30. About 16:00 plane from our field picked us up. Good to be home, even if it's Thurleigh, Eng. Carried 12- 500 lb. bombs. They blew up the officers- quarters at the airfield. Tired—to bed."

June 2. Clay Pidgeon. "Up at noon. Lunch, and briefed for a mission to Villacoublay, France. Marshalling yards and R.R. bridge. With Mac. We led high squadron in low group. No fighters. Lots of flak—mostly tracking. We got only one hole through right stabilizer. Many airfields smoking from other formations' bombs. We completely demolished the choke-point, and our ship's bombs destroyed the bridge. Ball-turret gunner followed our bombs. 12- 500 pounders. Target was just 2 miles south of Paris. Paris guns did not quite reach us. We bombed from 18,500'. 1700 gals. Gas. Tired. Mission lasted five hours. To bed."

June 17. Clay Pidgeons. "Up at 01:00. Briefed for mission to Paris. Mission scrubbed at 04:00. Back to bed. Up again at 08:00. Briefed on mission to Orleans, France. Mission all screwed up. Finally bombed bridge over rivers near LeMans, France. Mission lasted six hours. Dingman went down over French coast. Six chutes were seen come out. Also Pederson went down on way back. All chutes came out of his plane. #312 & #163. Now to bed."

June 20. Clay Pidgeon. "Up at 01:00. Waked up too late for briefing. Took off at 04:30. Went to Hamburg, Germany. Mission lasted 7-1/2 hours. 25,000' – 12-500 lb. bombs (demos). Bombed oil refineries and docks on south side of river. We flew #4 in lead sqdn. & lead group. After seeing the results, I would say offhand that Hamburg "has had it." Just a rubble in the town, anyway. Columns of smoke 20,000' high. The whole river ablaze. Never saw anything like it. An excellent job. Flak heavy—plenty close hits—but none hit us. Some shot up badly. 423rd lost two ships over target. Saw two F.W. 190s. Home and hit the sack... 16 missions now."

June 21. Clay Pidgeons. "Up at 24:00—in fact, I wasn't in bed yet. Went to Berlin today. Took off at 04:30. Mission lasted 10:50. A long haul. Intense contrails—formation scattered. Flak heavy but widely dispersed. Few enemy fighters. Many fires in Berlin—not much but a rubble now. 1500 Forts and Libs over it today. About 25 Combat Wings. Lancasters (900 of them) were supposed to follow us—but screwed up I guess. Many ships in trouble—ditching, etc. Not as bad as my first one, however. To bed. Need lots of rest. 17 missions now. I was pro-rated 3 missions—have to do 32 missions in my tour now."

July 17. Clay pidgeons. "Up at 02:00. Went on my first (F.C.M.) mission as first pilot. Crunican, Carter, Ristuccia, and Shaw from my regular crew. Good mission. #053. Bombed bridge over canal—hit it on the nose. Bridge near Ham, France. Sleep! Flew #5 in high squadron."

July 24. Clay Pidgeons. "Up at 02:00. Went on mission to Normandy front. Bombed troops, etc. Just like D-Day. Bombed from 15,000'. Visibility poor, but good results were obtained. Would hate to have been down there. We dropped 38- 100# bombs-demos. Little flak—good mission. Pleasure Bent has scavenger-pump trouble in #1, so we had to take #065. Rough!"

July 25. Clay Pidgeons. "Up at 02:00. Went on same mission as yesterday. Bombed the same places. The whole 8th A.F. out again. Also ninth A.F. with mediums and fighter-bombers. Little flak again. Bombed from 12,000'. Sitting ducks. Pleasure Bent in rare form. Painted "Emily" on fuselage this afternoon, and Carter painted "Florence." To bed."

July 31. Clay Pidgeons. "Up at 04:30. Went to Munich. Led high squadron in low group. Did fairly well for first time. Flak accurate tracking type. Our wing - #306th – led 8th A.F. today. General Turner went in lead ship. Deputy had to take over on bomb run-Tell. 09:40-long mission. Co-pilot was Fowler—1000 flying hours. His first mission. Six more. Wrote letters, & to bed."

August 13. Clay Pidgeons. "Up at 06:30. Bombed road on west side of Seine River west of Paris, to help trap 30 German divisions expected to retreat across Seine. Lots of accurate flak, but we got none in high sqdn. I led high sqdn. Saw 3 ships go down. Pretty good mission. Carried 38- 100 lb demos. Bombardier, Gruenig, had to chop one out that hung up. Wrote letters, & to bed."

One wonders how well RCS actually slept that night!

The 306th B.G. and the Clay Pigeons

During the years spanned by World War II, the Eighth Air Force contained over forty bombardment groups, one of which was the 306th. Constituted as the 306th Bombardment Group (Heavy) on January 28, 1942, activated on March 1 of that year, and later inactivated on December 25, 1946, the 306th was stationed for most of the war at Thurleigh, England, and was the longest serving bombardment group of the Eighth Air Force during this time.

Known as "the Reich Wreckers," the 306th consisted of four Bombardment Squadrons (Heavy) – the 367th, 368th, 369th, and 423rd – and flew mostly B17F and B17G combat aircraft on 341 completed missions between 1942 and 1945 while assigned to the 40th Combat Wing, First Air Division. Col. George L. Robinson was group CO from June 2, 1943, to September 23, 1944, during my father's tenure in Thurleigh as a member of the 367th B.S.

The 367th was named "The Clay Pigeons" for its record of sustaining the heaviest losses of any squadron in the Eighth Air Force from October 1942 through August 1943. Lt. Sage was proud to be part of this elite group despite its rather intimidating statistics, although losses for the Eighth Air Force decreased significantly by 1944 with the increase in long-range escorts (P-51s).

The 306th, including the Clay Pigeon squadron, participated in several operations to achieve air superiority over Europe. POINTBLANK (May 1943 – D-Day) was designed to support the invasion of Normandy (termed Operation OVERLORD). Because of the slow progress and incomplete success of POINTBLANK, another operation, ARGUMENT, was initiated (February 1944 – June 1944) to destroy the German aircraft industry (Westgate, 1998). My father was part of this effort, and the diary describes the missions and targets associated with the achievement of air superiority ensuring the success of the Allied invasion of Normandy. The loss of German fighter aircraft, the availability of long-range escorts, and the use of Pathfinder (PFF, a type of radar that enhanced bombing accuracy) contributed collectively to highly successful missions. Post-invasion objectives (July 1944 – April 1945) for the 306th included maintenance of air superiority and elimination of German support facilities that included oil production, transportation and airfields, and marshalling yards. Westgate (1998) points out that the loss of heavy bombers increased up to D-Day despite the general decline in loss rates sustained by the Eighth Air Force and the 306th B.G. during the progression of the war. The principal culprit was flak—from February to June 1944, 34% of the 1732 heavy bombers lost were taken out by anti-aircraft flak. The RCS diary contains some vivid descriptions of this menace, the only escape from which was due to luck. On August 16 the diary reports, "All planes in for repairs. Quite a bit of flak." In addition to bombs, the squadrons also occasionally dropped anti-German propaganda ("nickel"). History has indeed verified the critical role played by the 306th and its squadrons in the defeat of Nazi Germany.

The Flying Fortresses

Emmett Watson, a columnist for the *Seattle Times*, claimed that Boeing (located near Seattle) produced 6,981 of the 12,731 four-engine B17s that were manufactured for service during World War II. (Douglas and Lockheed manufactured the remaining aircraft.) Moreover, in the final year of the war, Boeing assembled 16 B17s every 24 hours. This prodigious output was in part a reflection of the substantial losses experienced by the Eighth Air Force.

The iconic status of the B-17 Flying Fortress was well-deserved. Used mostly by the U.S. Army Air Forces (AAF) for daylight bombing of German military installations and factories, it became famous for its potency in the air and its capacity to withstand severe damage (a feature much appreciated by those crewmen who returned safely to base). An interesting statistic is the tonnage of bombs dropped on Germany by B-17s: ~640,000 short tons are attributed to B-17s, of the total ~1,560,000 short tons by all U.S. aircraft (en.wikipedia.org).

In his diary, Lt. Sage mentions flying in no fewer than seven different aircraft ("ship numbers 053, 063, 065, 133, 278, 715-V, and 729"). Two of these were given names and personal decorations: #133 was known as "Pretty Baby"—a photograph of the pilot (my father), his crew, and the ship appears in Chapter 3. Ship #715-V was called "Pleasure Bent," with the pin-up style logo of a bowlegged cowgirl twirling a lariat (see cover). A conundrum arises in that "Pleasure Bent," with a different girlie logo, was part of the 838th Bombardment Squadron (a Boeing B-17G – 75-BO Fortress 43-37981) in 1944 (en.wikipedia.org, 11/24/2010). This was probably not the same ship flown by my father. Similar circumstances might apply to "Pretty Baby." The aircraft B-17G 42 (97133), part of the 367th B.S., transferred to the 91st B.G. on May 30, 1945, and later scrapped, was likely my father's ship (*Heavy Bombers of the Mighty Eighth, B17 Flying Fortress Story*). However, John Rogers, co-pilot of a B-17 also called "Pretty Baby," was shot down on February 24, 1944, and became a Prisoner of War (Stalag Luft I) (www.merkki.com, 11/24/2010). It is unlikely that this Pretty Baby and my father's ship were the same aircraft, as he reports flying "his" Pretty Baby months after the February crash.

The diary is rife with colorful details of the missions flown and the people involved therein, as well as everyday experiences of life on the base at Thurleigh and off the base on leave. The Standbridge Earls rest home makes for interesting reading and was clearly appreciated as a place where one might, at long last, rest. Incidentally, a lifelong attachment to horses (hunters) and riding began here for my father, who with no previous equestrian experience, "rode" a hunter over a steeplechase course, obviously out of control but with great enjoyment.

My father's gift to me, and more importantly to his country, in the form of this heretofore unknown diary, which was effectively buried for nearly 60 years, represents a critical part of his life as Lt. Robert C. Sage, D.F.C. It also honors all those members of the Eighth Air Force whose courageous and unselfish dedication contributed to the silencing of the Luftwaffe and the defeat of the Third Reich.

I

Robert C. Sage
The Early Years (1921-1943)

Flag Day – June 14 – an appropriate day for my father's birthday, and one he commemorated in later years with a full-masted American flag in his front yard (complete with a flood light when he was unable to lower it promptly at dusk). Robert Charles Sage was born in the year 1921 to Emily and Harry Ransley Sage, of Philadelphia, Pennsylvania. Although initially of modest means, his father, who had served in France in World War I, eventually became President of the Mutual Rendering Company of Philadelphia and was able to raise his two sons (Harry Russell Sage was born seven years later) in a post-war atmosphere of affluence. Early photographs show a robust little boy "Bobbie," in period costume and in an unidentified uniform (pages 15-16). The two brothers, shown on pages 17 and 18 in contrasting shorts (Harry) and long pants (Bob), grew up in the city, but spent summers at camp and the New Jersey seashore. Life overall was good, with an indulgent governess and a patient maid whose freshly-laundered white shirts my father delighted in hosing down. Education, denied their parents, was emphasized. After graduation from Frankfurt High School (page 19), Bob enrolled in Franklin and Marshall College; later, Harry attended Princeton University.

The landscape of relative comfort and security eroded quickly with the declaration of war by the United States against Japan and the Axis Powers on December 8 and 11, respectively, 1941. My father enlisted at the end of his freshman year and later became a Lieutenant, Air Forces, Army of the United States (p 19). Table 1 lists the locations and chronology of his military service.

RCS as a young boy in Philadelphia, Pennsylvania, c1924.

A few years later, RCS wears an unidentified uniform—Philadelphia (Olney) in the background, c1928.

RCS (*left*) and his brother, Harry Russell Sage (*right*), in their whites, possibly at a resort, c1932.

RCS (*right*) and brother Harry Russell (*lcft*), in their formal attire, with their Irish setter Sandy, c1935.

RCS, a high school graduation photograph (?), c1938.

ROBERT C. SAGE

LIEUTENANT, AIR FORCES
ARMY OF THE UNITED STATES

Air Forces, Army of the United States—card issued to Lt. Robert C. Sage.

II

Pilot Flight Record and Log Book (1943)
Combat Crew Training (1944)

My father's Pilot Flight record and Log Book begins on June 1, 1943, in Decatur, Alabama. On May 16, 1943, his family traveled with him to Alabama (*see* pp 22-23). That they were proud of him as a son and a soldier is evident in several photographs taken less than one year before his departure for England as a member of the Eighth Air Force (*see* pp 24-25). Within the year, Emily Sage (his mother and my grandmother, p 26) would send him a photograph of her arrangement of his mementos (his photograph, flags, and officer's hat) captioned: "Thinking of you, Robert" (p 27).

This small bound book (7-1/4" L x 4-1/4" W) was issued by the Aero Service & Supply Company/Municipal Airport/Birmingham, Alabama. The first page provides for the pilot's name, address, and vital statistics: SAGE, Robert C., 4830 Castor Avenue, Philadelphia, Pennsylvania. Birthdate: June 14, 1921; Height: 6'0"; Color Hair: Blond; Color Eyes: Blue; Weight: 145#; Remarks: None. The first entry occurred on June 1, 1943, at Decatur, Alabama, a local flight in a Stearman PT-17, with descriptive notes following flights on successive days (e.g., stalls, spins, S turns, 180° turns, landings, takeoffs, and glides). The entire logbook has been reproduced in Appendix A. It is a precise documentation of my father's flight training and experience that ended on December 2, 1943.

His first solo occurred on June 17, a local flight from Decatur, in the Stearman PT-17; it lasted 24 minutes ("First solo! Storm came up."). Beginning on July 17, longer flights in the Stearman are recorded (Cullman-Arab and return; Hartselle to Guntersville Dam and return). July 23 was a special day: "60 hr. check. Passed! Mr. Lundy." In August he has begun to fly locally out of Courtland, Alabama, in a Vultee-BT 13A, with a first solo on August 11. Night flying is recorded with flood and wing lights in early September, and with no lights on September 10. Towns in this interval (with returns) included Jack's Creek to Corinth, Aberdeen to Jasper, Oxford, Graham to Corinth, and Crossville to Smithville. A photograph dated 9/11/1943 shows "Sage, Emme, Johnson, Phila. boys – BT 13A Vultee – Vibrator #444, Squadron I – Flight A" (*see* p 28, top). After a 40-hour check on September 22 (Lt. R.C. Moore), there was further practice in cross-country and acrobatics, ending with a sign-out on September 28.

Seymour, Indiana, was the final base for my father's flight training, from October 7 to December 2, 1943. In a Beechcraft AT10, he flew formation and accrued hours in formation, cross-country navigation, and night flying. Destinations included Rushville, Terre Haute, Richmond, Princeton, and Lexington. Longer flights were recorded in November, from Walnut Ridge to Monroe, Louisiana, from Selman Field, Louisiana, to Courtland, Alabama, and other destinations from Seymour to Muncie, Terre Haute, Richmond, Indianapolis, Effingham, Lafayette, Danville, Evansville, Walesboro, Louisville, and Fort Wayne, many of which were night excursions.

On later pages are recorded "Primary," "Basic," and "Advanced" stages in a Link Trainer aircraft: "July 1943 – S.A.T.S./Decatur, Ala. ('Primary'); Aug. 3-31 – C.A.A.F./ Courtland, Ala.('Basic'); Sept. 6-C.A.A.F./Courtland, Ala. (Radio Completed for 'Basic'); October 7-26 – Freeman Field/Seymour, Ind. ('Advanced' 1-hour lecture on radio)."

Combat Crew Training (1944)

Combat Crew training (B-17) commenced in Dalhart, Texas, in early 1944. Despite few comments about his experiences in World War II, this western town clearly made a strong impression on both my parents, as it crept into isolated conversations over succeeding years. The major city of the Dust Bowl of the 1930s, Dalhart was known in the preceding decade as the "City on the High Plains" and boasted, by 1929, an influential newspaper (the *Dalhart Texan*), two railroad accesses, a primitive airplane landing strip, and over 4000 inhabitants (Egan, 2006). With a major proportion of the native sod overturned and the grasses sacrificed largely to wheat farming, coupled with the Great Depression, bank failures, grasshopper plagues, a decade of horrendous drought, and extremes of temperature, Dalhart all but essentially died. Even to this day, Timothy Egan describes it as "a windblown and dog-eared town at the crossroads of three highways" (2006). The picture must have been more desolate in 1944. The images on page 28 (bottom) and 29 (top) show a small western town with a café, drugstore, hardware store, gas station, and Masonic temple. Helen Daumann (Mrs. Robert Charles Sage) adopted both a Western look, with a pair of cowboy boots, and a military look, with cap, shirt, and wings (p 29, bottom). The English jodhpurs are suggestive of some horseback riding in, what was for her, a lonely, dusty place. My father, sitting on the same fence, is dressed warmly in rather casual military attire (p 30).

This handsome couple was married on December 11, 1943, shortly after his acceptance of a commission and combat training prior to an overseas tour of duty. RCS is in uniform and appears more confident than Helen, who wears orchids and appears wistful (p 31).

The family gathered once again to see RCS off for his tour of duty in the European Theater. In photographs from Kansas City dated March 1944, a youthful Lt. Robert Sage and his wife Helen stand together (perhaps, in their minds, for the last time) (pp 32-33).

At the train station, his mother, father, and Helen posed together (p 34). A particularly sensitive photograph shows RCS and his mother at this location (p 35). He was later to record in his diary from England (Chapter 3) no less than 46 letters to his "folks" and 72 to Helen, none of which appears to have survived.

My mother left Beaver College during wartime and was, for a brief interval, Albert Einstein's secretary at Princeton University. Unfortunately, few details of this experience were recorded.

Family photograph, Alabama, dated May 16, 1943. *Left* to *right*: Harry Russell, Emily (mother), RCS, and Harry Ransley (father).

"My Son Robert" – Alabama, May, 1943.

Family photo – *Left* to *right*: Harry (father), Emily (mother), RCS in uniform, and Harry Russell (brother), 1943.

RCS in uniform and pipe – standing in front of an hotel, possibly Alabama, 1943.

RCS with his mother, Emily Moleton Sage. Cold weather here.

Memento of her son during 1944 – *verso*: "Thinking of you, Robert." Note photography, hat, and flags.

Trainees - *left* to *right*: "Sage, Emme, Johnson, Phila. boys. BT 13A Vultee – Vibrator #444. Squadron I, Flight A", inscribed in RCS's handwriting *verso*.

Dalhart, Texas, 1944, B-17 Combat Crew Training base.

Dalhart, Texas-Main Street, 1944.

Ella Helen Daumann (Mrs. Robert C.) Sage, Dalhart, Texas, 1944, in mixed uniform.

RCS, Dalhart, Texas, 1944.

Helen D. (the author's mother) and Robert C. Sage, wedding photograph, December 11, 1943, Kansas City, March, 1944.

RCS in uniform, Kansas City, March, 1944.

RCS and his wife Helen, Kansas City, March, 1944.

Family photograph, probably in Kansas City, 1944. *Left* to *right*: Helen, Harry, and Emily Sage, and RCS.

Farewell between mother and son, 1944: Emily in fur coat (*left*) and RCS (*right*).

III

The Diary
April 12, 1944, to September 7, 1944

The diary is handwritten in fountain pen ink, with entries extending from April 2 to September 7, 1944. A complete record of missions flown by RCS appears in tabular form on the final two pages. This list appears in Appendix B. The diary is missing its hard covers, but the binding and pages are intact; pages other than April 2 through September 7 are blank. The size of the diary, 5-1/8" x 4-1/8", allowed its concealment, as the keeping of diaries at this time was discouraged.

The last entry appears on the first page (January 5): "To be delivered by Dianne, safely to E. Helene Sage at my death, if not sooner. [signed] R.C. Sage, 4/16/2001." Dianne was his wife at this time. I received the diary approximately one year later and soon after his death in 2002.

The first photo on page 68 serves as an introduction to the ship "Pretty Baby" and its crew. The photograph was taken shortly after a practice formation flight around England at an altitude of 400'. My father, grinning, stands in the middle of the back row. His co-pilot was identified as Fowler (RCS wrote that Fowler flew with him twice, and that "we experienced shortages of personnel from time to time"). Also standing in the back row (left to right) are Charles Crunican (bombardier), Fred Lauer (tail gunner), and Don Carter (top turret gunner and flight engineer). Kneeling (left to right) are Ralph Shaw (ball turret gunner), Ed Ronczy (navigator), Larry Ristuccia (left waist gunner), unidentified (this man replaced Everett Malan, who was wounded and hospitalized), and Ed (Dick) Dickhaus (right waist gunner). These individuals recur throughout the diary and were clearly an important part of my father's military life. Flight missions attendant with casualties, as seen in my father's wartime photograph collection (pp 69 and 70 (top)), were part of everyday life for these men.

Prior to his arrival in England, the diary describes four feet of snow in Goose Bay, Labrador, and the "no-man's land" of Meeks Field, Keflavik, Iceland (p 70, bottom). Stone, England (Beattie Hall) receives some "cultural" entries (April 14-18), where RCS met local inhabitants, including members of the W.A.A.F. and the Women's Land Army, tasted English beer, censored enlisted men's mail, and rode bicycles (p 71). These activities preceded early training at Bovingdon ("don't care much for this place") and final stationing at Thurleigh, England (Station 111), on April 28 ("We're in Eighth Air Force now", p 72).

On May 15, 1944, RCS "flew on gunnery mission" in the morning and later inspected his newly-assigned ship #065, which he described as "pretty well shot up." Photographs dated on that day are shown on pages 73 and 74, and contemporaneous vignettes with his "ship" (probably #065), fellow officers, and Don Carter appear on pages 75 through 78.

June 14 marked my father's 23rd birthday ("23 years—feel older") and, coincidentally, a day of photography at the Link Trainer Dept. These photos, inscribed "Link Trainer, June 14, 1944, Clay Pidgeon Squadron, to my best girl, Ellie" and "To my sweet wife," are shown on pages 79 through 81.

Missions in which my father was involved began on May 8 (Berlin), and were concentrated over June and the latter part of July. The final mission, #29, was flown on August 24 over Merseburg, Germany (see Appendix B). The diary entries over this interval are compelling and contribute interesting information on Clay Pigeon activity.

Eventually RCS was sent on "flak leave" during the first week of August. The rest home was a beautiful English mansion, Standbridge Earls, Romsey, Hants (seven miles northeast of Southampton, see page 82). A formal photograph of him with his flight engineer, Don Carter, on which is written the name of the rest home and the ages of the two young men ("22 and 23 respectively") has been reproduced on page 83. Clearly this rest was indicated (most of the diary entries over this week are blank). RCS, with golf club in hand (page 84), was taken with the "view from my room of rear of English house" and especially with "the home of the 'egg girl'—she was lovely!" (see page 85).

After his 29th mission, my father reports that he is "in hospital on a little rest cure," and by September 1 he was "kicked out of hospital today. Also taken off combat. Going home they say. Wonderful." One can only imagine the emotion that has crept to the surface of this diary entry. The now "kiwi-paddlefoot or groundgripper" ended his diary on September 30, 1944.

A poem written by my mother to RCS on V-J Day (August 15, 1945) has been reproduced on page 86.

Footnotes pertaining to most entries have been included at the end of the diary.

LIEUT. ROBERT C. SAGE, D.F.C., AIR FORCES,
ARMY OF THE UNITED STATES
FLIGHT DIARY, APRIL 2 – SEPT. 7, 1944.

April 2. Kearney A. A. F., Kearney, Neb. "Said g'bye to Ellie at 6:40 A.M. Called her again at noon. Called home at 5P.M. all there! We went to bed at 8:30 P.M. & arose at 2:30. Took off at 8:00 A.M. Long trip Overeast up to 14,000'. Arrived Bangor 5:15 P.M."

April 4. Dow Field, Bangor, Me. "Processed until 8P.M. Then ate. I went over to Club. Had two beers and came back. After shower & shave, to bed. Up tomorrow at 6 A.M. Lots of trees here. And I'm damned tired!"

April 5. Dow Field, Bangor, Me. "Got up at 7:30-ate breakfast-good chow here. Slept all day. Wrote letter #1 to Helen & folks. Went to bed early. Had briefing at 19:30."

April 6. Dow Field, Bangor, Me. "Got up at 7:00-breakfast-went to ship but radio compass not fixed yet. Back to barracks. Slept all afternoon. Took walk with Nielsen, Reynolds, & Carlson up through woods. Stopped in hospital. Nice post. Went to P.X.-ate sirloin steak-good-and drank beer with Lauer-our tail-gunner. To bed at 23:00-Crunican came in drunk."

April 7. Dow Field, Bangor, Me. "Got up at 7:30-breakfast. Reported for take-off-takeoffs cancelled for today. Good deal. Played cards until 14:00-had sirloin steak-went to Church for 10 mins. Wrote Helen letter #2. Went over fence into Bangor. Nice town."

April 8. Goose Bay, Labrador. "Got up at 7:00-ate breakfast-slept until 9:00-took off from Bangor (Dow Field) for Goose Bay, Labrador. Arrived there 16:00. Nice place. Four feet of snow. Ate & slept-played cards with Ronny & Chuck. Got ready for takeoff at 24:00."

April 9. Easter. Meeks Field, Kaflavik, Iceland. "Had engine trouble-didn't take off for Meeks Field, Iceland, until 06:30 G.M.T. Overcast all the way-saw some of the Atlantic-Got four hours actual instrument time. Landed Iceland at 16:30 G.M.T. What a hole-unbelievable. Huts half-buried in the ground-no trees. Big mount mud & stones. Poor food-fellows stationed here are wacky-been here too long. Fox holes-barbed wire fences. Looks like "no-man's land." Well, I'm in a "hut" on a cot. One comforter, and not too comforting either. It is 19:40 G.M.T.-brief tomorrow morning. Just can't write home tonight. I'm just too tired. They say they've been attacked couple times.Tanker strafed & bombed here lately. Well, to bed. (Iceland's money-Eyrir=1/10 cent. Auran=1 cent. Kronur=15 cents."

April 10. Easter Monday. Meeks Field, Kaflavik, Iceland. Letter #5 to Helen-#2 to folks. "Up at 08:30 this morning. What a sleep! Clothes on-shoes & all. Well rested now. We ate breakfast, taxied ship to new place-and then went to village-2 miles away-of Kaflavik. About 500 pop. People pro-nazi. Ignored us. Children speak English fairly. Ask for pennies & chewing gum. Were interested in map I had of U.S. Nothing at all in village. Just fishermen. British tanker Basset Hound unloading oil. Lots of fishing boats. Dirty place. Fish heads all over peoples' back yards. Cod fish mostly. New cars. Mostly with wheel on right side. People very fair. Pretty girls, but they walk like men. Stores closed. Holiday. Probably take off for Scotland tomorrow. If not, will go to Reykjavik-about 30 miles from the village. Talked to Red Cross girl for few minutes. Been here 16 mos. Brave kid. I know I'd go nuts. Nothing at all to do. Men here rationed U.S. beer. Lots of inflation here. People speak Icelandic language. Sent 5 Kronurs home. Worth 77 cents. Well, to bed again."

April 11. Nutts Corner, Northern Ireland. Near Belfast-12 mi. "We had a wonderful trip from Iceland to here, via Stornoway, Scotland. We took off at 13:00, arrived here 19:05. They took Dingy-Dingy I from us. Ate supper at R.A.F. mess-fairly good. Had couple beers & stouts at R.A.F. Pub. Retired to lounge 'til 01:30- fireplace, etc. Very restful-and British. Saw three convoys today. Scottish coastline beautiful. Irish countryside cannot be equaled. Towns so neat from the air. Changed $123.40 into British money at mess hall. L (pounds sterling symbol) 5.0. Huts are not bad living in. Ready for bed now. Very tired."

April 12. Nutts Corner, Northern Ireland. Wednesday. "They forgot to wake us this A.M. Got up at 13:00-had lunch at R.A.F. mess. Good food. Better than U.S. More tasty. Good cheese. Played Snooker with the boys all afternoon. Had tea & cakes at 17:00, then supper at 19:00, then beer and Irish Whisky all evening at their "Pub". The R.A.F. base C.O. was a "capital chap". Mixed with us, kept up quite a party. Group Leader he was. Same as our full Col. They are wonderful people. I like them very well.They were of the upper class, however. Were several W.A.A.F.'s there also. Well-mannered, reserved people. I had late tea and fish & cheese with an enlisted R.A.F. man. Game of chess too. Got beaten. In bed at 04:00. Very tired!"

April 13. Thursday. On train enroute to Stone, England. "This is a cold, but not too bad a ride. We left Nutts Corner by truck at 10:00, arrived, boarded train for, got off after 3 ½ hours at, got on transport ship, took us to Stramar(sp?), Scotland, went to R.A.F. fatigue camp, had supper, and drank good English beer at Officer's club in an AnteRoom. Fireplaces, etc.-very comfortable and relaxing. Boarded train at 24:00. Riding now. Blackout all over the Isles, of course. We are bound for somewhere in England. Stone is the town. I'll try to get some sleep. All four of us in this compartment."

April 14. Friday. Beattie Hall, Stone, England. Sent cablegram. "We arrived here at 10:00. This A.M. saw some ruins from Jerries' bombs. These people know what war is. The people at home don't know a damn thing about it. We processed, etc. ate lunch-food is fair. I got my P.X. rations. 12 cigars, can pipe tobacco,cake soap, matches, bar of cheap chocolate, package of chewing gum. Must last for one week. No place to get milkshakes or sandwiches, etc. No such thing here. Can get English beer at club here at night. Chuck and I borrowed one bicycle and went into stone tonight. Went to the Crown Hotel. Poor service. Talked to two Limie girls. Very stupid. Middle class. Pub closed at 22:00. Came home in rain. Ready for bed. No sheets. Nice air here. Not too cold."

April 15. Saturday. Beattie Hall, Stone, England. "Up at 7:30. Too late for breakfast. Orientation lecture at 09:00. Good film on introduction to U.K. Ate lunch, took grip to be fixed, and went to Gas lecture. Issued new masks. Fell asleep until supper time. Ate supper, shaved, and went to club. Drank them out of beer, and turned in about 24:00, quite tired again."

April 16. Sunday. Beattie Hall, Stone, England. "Up at 7:30, poor breakfast, cleaned room and reported to censoring room. Censored enlisted men's mail for two hours. Some really have "tales of woe". Chuck & I got bicycles, and at 13:00 started on our way for Hamley, Stoke-on-Trent, Staffordshire. We stopped at Filleybrook's Pub. 'til they closed at 14:00, then proceeded to Hamley. We walked all over the place, ate sandwiches at Red Cross, and then went to Grand Hotel. Later went to couple other Pubs. Drank beer & stout. Talked to couple W.A.A.F.'s. Also saw couple from Women's Land Army. They work on farms, etc. Pubs close at 22:00. Black-outs are really black-outs here. You can't even see other side of the street. Few autos. People walk in streets, everywhere. Singing, laughing. They are gay for five years of war. Hamley was bombed 3 times. They are a good people. To bed."

April 17. Monday. Beattie Hall, Stone, England. Letter #4 to Helen. Letter #3 to folks. " Still here! Slept until 16:00. Got up for supper, washed 35 hkdfs. Wrote letters, went over to club, had one mug of beer, met Peters, Sandlin, & Cusick. Mehmer no doubt lost. Came back, shaved, showered & to bed."

April 18. Tuesday. Beattie Hall, Stone, Stoke-on-Trent, Staff., Eng. Letter #5 to Helen. "Got up for breakfast, censored mail, cleared post, and went to Hamley with Mac. Had Scotch & beer, returned in taxi, without Mac. And to bed."

April 19. Wednesday. Bovingdon, Eng. (about 25 miles from London) (15 miles from Watford). "Boarded train at Stone about 16:00. Arrived here 19:30. Got off train at Boxmoor. Came here by truck. This is a rough and ready place. Very combat-like. Learn more about it tomorrow. Poor quarters. Tired!"

April 20. Thursday. Bovingdon, Eng. Letter #6 to Helen. "Don't care very much for this place. Poor living quarters. Food is fair. Told us today we have 30 missions to do. We're in Eighth Air Force now. Orientation lecture at 08:00. Beer tonight and then good supper. Started for London, but someone stole taxi from us. Now 21:00- Ready for bed. Lots of formations went over tonight. Must be a raid on Berlin. This field is the Germans' I.P. for London. Could be a hot spot. B.B.C. News is on now. To bed. – P.S. Oh yes, I met Joe Tunstall this A.M. He is leaving here tomorrow. Going to the 308th Bomb Group. Mac & I put in today for the 91st, 306th, 92nd Groups. The oldest ones."

April 21. Bovingdon, England. "Got up for breakfast-school all day. Left here for London at 18:00. Taxi to Watford, train to Piccadilly Circus, London. Ate dinner at Piccadilly Hotel, then Rick's Club, etc. Nice big city. Saw bombed houses and church. Odd taxicabs there. Got back here at 07:15, and couldn't stay awake in class all day. Played cards with boys until 22:00, few beers, and now bed."

April 22. Bovingdon, England. "Continued" (arrow from April 21 page but this page is blank).

April 23. Bovingdon, England. Letter #4 to folks. Letter #7 to Helen. "Up for breakfast. Fresh fried eggs! Wonderful. School all day. Nothing exciting. Ate supper and played "Hearts" with Chuck, Mac, & Sandy. Drank beer with Chuck until 23:00. Back to bed."

April 24. Bovingdon, England. Letter #8 to Helen." Missed breakfast. Too tired. Got P.X. rations. Pineapple juice good, 12 cigars, 1 Hershey bar, 1 pack gum, 2 boxes matches. Must look up Ross's Group when I get to mine. 389th he was in. Supper poor tonite. Going up now to shave and wash a bit. No mail yet. Wrote letter to Helen after shaving, and now to bed."

April 25. Bovingdon, England. "Nothing exciting-nothing new. Same old routine. Tired-to bed."

April 26. Bovingdon, England. "Nothing new again. Tired-to bed."

April 27. Bovingdon, England. "Mac & I took off for London. Good time- slept at Coventry Court Hotel. Went to Piccadilly again. Omelette for supper. Later to Blue Lagoon night-club. A rugged night. Good breakfast at the Piccadilly-tea for breakfast too."

April 28. 367th Bomb Sqdn. 306th Bomb Group (H). A.P.O. 557, Thurleigh, Eng. 7 miles from Bedford. "Returned to base this A.M. at 10:30. Got on train at 14:30, arrived at Bedford at 17:00. Looks like a nice town. This base looks O.K. But it's late-to bed."

April 29. Clay Pidgeon. Letter #9 to Helen. "Well, we got up at 08:00, had breakfast, went to school until 11:00, ate lunch-very good incidentally-went to school from 14:00 to 15:00-then we were through for the day. Good bunch of boys here. Damned good. The 67th was stood down today. Group raided Berlin today. One lost in group. 63 all together I think. Drank beer with gang at club tonight. A riot. Had a swell time. Shaved-and to bed."

April 30. Clay Pidgeons. Letter #5 to folks. Letter #10 to Helen. "Up at 07:45-good breakfast-security lecture from 09:00 to 11:00-good lunch. Lectures 14:00 to 16:00-shower-good supper. Three beers & bed. The boys raided Lyons, France airfield today."

May 1. Clay Pidgeon. "Up for breakfast-no school-good deal. Scotch before supper-bed after supper."

May 2. Clay Pidgeon. "Up at 07:30-breakfast-combat-meeting at 08:30- engine operation lecture- lunch-combat meeting at 13:15-paid-hospital-etc. Went into town at 17:00-nice place (Bedford). Ate supper and washed at Red Cross Officers' Club. A very nice and pleasant environment. Bought bicycle for 5 L (pounds sterling) 10 s . Met Tunstall by chance-had few beers-looked the place over- got on truck at 23:15- and to bed."

May 3. Clay Pidgeon. Letter #6 to folks. Letter #11 to Helen. "Up at 08:00-breakfast-Mac flew practice mission. Nothing to do all day. Wrote letters-to bed."

May 4. Clay Pidgeon. "Up at usual time-flew two hours with "Slim"Somerville. Hard country to do pilotage. Had one hour link-trainer-Lorenz system. Did very well. Played black-jack all evening with enlisted-men. Then to bed."

May 5. Clay Pidgeon. Letter #12 to Helen. "Flew two hours low altitude formation this morning. Matichka was pilot. Lunch and 2 hours tactics lecture by Col. Raper-air executive officer. Took shower & shaved- then supper. Fish tonight! Wrote letter-had snacks at club-one beer-and to bed."

May 6. Clay Pidgeon. Letter #7 to folks. Letter #13 to Helen. "Up for breakfast-flew from 10:30 to 15:45 gunnery mission. Low alt. formation. Tow target never showed up. Plenty tired. Received 8 letters. First mail received. Wrote letters and to bed."

May 7. Clay Pidgeons. "Up at 8:00-missed breakfast. Chuck & Mac went on Berlin raid. All planes returned, but ship Chuck was on got in ½ hour late. Shot up from flak. Heavy flak they said. No fighters. Received 11 letters. One from Mrs. Ross. I went on two practice missions. Tired tonight. Shaved, ½ hours B.J. with enlisted men-and to bed."

May 8. Clay Pidgeon. "Up at 01:30 this morning. Briefed at 03:00. Went to Berlin. Took off at 06:15. Arrived target about 11:00. We dropped behind formation. Salvoed bombs to catch up. Poor engines. Not too much flak. No fighters. Carried 10- 500 lbs. bombs. Also chaff. Saw 3 ships collide and blow up immediately in front of us. Not too crazy about this stuff. Flak pretty accurate. Cloud cover-bombed by PFF. Letter from Dad here. Sleep-sleep-sleep. P.S. Our own fighter support was good. The three ships lost were from our squadron. Five from our group. Took 9 hrs. 40 min. -47 degrees. Nearly froze. No heater. Flak hole in right wing, outside #4 engine. Everybody O.K. Flew over Amsterdam on return."

May 9. Clay Pidgeon. Letter #14 to Helen. "Up at 02:15-flew as spare on mission to Thionville, airfield and marshalling yards. Left the formation at mid-channel. No abortions. No ships lost. Little flak & no fighters. No mail today. Very tired. To bed."

May 10. Clay Pidgeon. Letter #15 to Helen. Letter #8 to folks. "Up for breakfast at 02:00. Briefed for mission to airdrome in northern Germany. Took off at 06:15. Weather bad, airplanes milling around all over the sky. Mission called off at 09:30. Returned to base at 10:00. Slept all day until supper. Talked to Tunstall for awhile, wrote letters, and to bed. Received 14 letters today."

May 11. Clay Pidgeon. "Up at 02:00. Flew as spare on mission to Saarbrucken. Turned back at mid-channel. Boys had a pretty tough raid. We were assigned #053- it failed to return here- but they got to the English coast allright. Received letter from Dad today. Tired-to bed."

May 12. Clay Pidgeon. "Up at 01:40. Briefing at 02:00. We went to Merseburg, Germany, and bombed the Leuna Oil Plant. Produces 600,000 gals. Synthetic aviation gasoline yearly. We blew the hell out of it. Huge fires & black columns of black smoke We had old #729- open waist windows. Ristuccia & Dickhaus were both frost-bitten on the face. Not a flak-hole. We flew #6 in high squadron. Tired-to bed. Received letter from Mother."

May 13. Clay Pidgeon. "Up at 05:00. Briefed at 06:00. Went on raid to bomb Stettin, in old Poland. Bombed PFF. An 11 hour haul. Flew over Denmark, and just South of Sweden. We flew #3 in lead sqdn. & lead groups, on Col. Raper's left wing. PFF ship. Very heavy flak. We had at least 30 holes in our plane. Flak was very accurate, also. One piece came in under windshield & hit steering column and up & out other side of cockpit. Another piece through side, inch behind my foot, down thru floor. Plenty rough. #4, new ship, ditched. All men saved. Our ship #278, its first mission, full of holes. Rough one. Received letter from Rentschler. To bed-exhausted."

May 14. Clay Pidgeon. Letter #16 to Helen. Letter # 9 to folks. "Slept until 10:30. "Stood down" today. Flew this afternoon on test flight for one hour. Wrote letters-and to bed. 3 missions in now."

May 15. Clay Pidgeon. Letter #17 to Helen. "Flew on gunnery mission this morning. One hour of ground school this afternoon, then went out to look at our newly assigned ship, #065. Pretty well shot up. Received 3 letters from Helen today, and one from Dad. Tired-shaved and to bed."

May 16. Clay Pidgeon. Letter #18 to Helen. "Up at 08:15. Missed breakfast. Ground school all morning and afternoon. Link Trainer operator knew Parnes. Went down on his first mission. Bombardier. Met Peters tonight- squadron commander upperclass at Maxwell Field. Talked over Zombie days. To bed. Probably a mission tomorrow."

May 17. Clay Pidgeon. Letter #10 to folks. Letter #19 to Helen. "Up at 02:30-briefed for mission to Stade, but mission was "scrubbed" at taxi time. Back in the sack until noon. Combat meeting at 13:15, and movie "Memphis Belle" at 14:00. Wrote letters, and to bed."

May 18. Clay Pidgeon. "Up at 08:15-missed breakfast. Supposed to go on pass, but it was cancelled. Received letter from Ryan & Mother today. Link Trainer this afternoon. To bed. Should go on pass tomorrow at noon, but maybe a mission instead."

May 19. Clay Pidgeon. London. "Flew gunnery mission until 12:30. Went on pass to London with Mac & Ronczy. Stayed at Imperial Hotel. Met Bill Grey at the American Bar. Ate supper at Carlton Grille, met him again at New Ambassador Club (Mrs. Platt the actress)- and proceeded to Cocoanut Grove. Lots of Scotch and good evening. British paratroop Major at Ritz Hotel Dolphin Square. Train ride."

May 20. Clay Pidgeon. London. "Slept practically all day. Had supper. New Ambassador & Cocoanut Grove again. Gin! Good night."

May 21. Clay Pidgeon. London. "Slept late. Beer for breakfast at Pub. Long walk through Battersea Park. Ate ham & sandwiches there also. Tea later. Relaxed until train time. Barely made it at Pancrast (sic) Station, 20:15. Ate supper at Red Cross, arrived Thurleigh at 11:45. Tired out!"

May 22. Clay Pidgeon. Letter #20 to Helen. "Up at 3:30. Went on raid to Kiel. Regular crew. Our own ship now #063. Shot up a little by flak. About 10 holes. Not too bad a mission. Tired. To bed. PFF ship went down."

May 23. Clay Pidgeon. Letter #11 to folks. "Up at 03:00. Went on raid to Saarbrucken, but we 'aborted' about ½ hour before I.P. With Allen's crew . Crunican was along. #4 engine caught fire, turned back, engine wouldn't feather, fire went out. We let down to 10,000 ft. on top of cloud-deck, few minutes four beautiful P51's escorted us all the way home. Two P47's looked us over too. Three engines got us home O.K. We salvoed our bombs "safe" over France to lighten load. Flak picked us up on the way out. About ten holes. Chuck had his hand splintered with plexi-glass. Probably Purple Heart. Not seriously injured. I'm exhausted. Slept all afternoon. To bed again."

May 24. Clay Pidgeon. Letter #21 to Helen. "Up at 08:00. Breakfast & combat meeting. Flew gunnery mission. Good mission. The other squadrons went to Berlin today. Now for bed again."

May 25. Clay Pidgeon. "Up at 03:00. Flew "spare" on mission to Thionville marshalling yards. Back in bed at 11:00. Tough war. Slept all day."

May 26. Clay Pidgeon. "Up at 08:00. Fresh fried eggs for breakfast. Nothing all morning. Flew practice formation in afternoon. Still tired. To bed."

May 27. Clay Pidgeon. Letter #22 to Helen. Letter #12 to folks. "Up at 08:00. Nothing to do all morning. Went to combat meeting at 1:15. No duty, so went to Bedford. Need coupons to buy clothes, etc. Bought nothing. Went to 'Key Club', and home on 23:15 'Liberty Run.' Bed."

May 28. Clay Pidgeon. "Up at 02:00. Briefed on raid to Ruhland. Synthetic Oil Refinery plant there. 8 ½ hour run. Little flak-no fighters. Ruhland is S-SE of Berlin. Saw fires all over Germany. Tired-to bed. Six missions now!"

May 29. Clay Pidgeon. Letter 323 to Helen. "Up at 08:00. Flew practice formation mission in morning. Another in afternoon. Tired. To bed."

May 30. Clay Pidgeon. "Briefed for mission to Berneberg, Ger. Mission was scrubbed because of weather at Berneberg. I was flying with Malsom. Nothing new. To bed."

May 31. Clay Pidgeon. "Went to Airfield at Liege, Belgium. Made three runs over target. We salvoed our bombs on last run. I was with Malsom. Lost #4 engine on first run, hit #3 on second run. Feathered both engines and came home alone on two engines. Towering cumulus clouds-rime-ice. Piece flak size of a baseball came through floor under my left foot, and out my side under window. Expected to ditch, but did not have to. Made R.A.F. field on English coast. Landed at 12:30. About 16:00 plane from our field picked us up. Good to be home, even if it's Thurleigh, Eng. Carried 12- 500 lb. bombs. They blew up the officers-quarters at the airfield. Tired- to bed."

June 1. Clay Pidgeon. Letter #13 to folks. Letter #24 to Helen. "Up at 08:15. Ground school. Flew practice formation all afternoon. Nothing new. To bed."

June 2. Clay Pidgeon. "Up at noon. Lunch, and briefed for a mission to Villacoublay, France. Marshalling yards & R.R. bridge. With Mac. We led high squadron in low group. No fighters. Lots of flak- mostly tracking. We got only one hole thru right stabilizer. Many airfields smoking from other formations' bombs. We completely demolished the choke-point, and <u>our</u> ship's bombs destroyed the bridge. Ball-turret gunner followed our bombs. 12- 500 pounders. Target was just 2 miles south of Paris. Paris guns did not quite reach us. We bombed from 18,500'. 1700 gals. Gas. Tired. Mission lasted five hours. To bed."

June 3. Clay Pidgeon. Letter #14 to folks. Letter #25 to Helen. "Up at 11:00. Ground school and out to dispersal area for awhile. Our ship was flown by Dingman yesterday. Shot up pretty badly. In hangar now. To bed at 23:00. Gran-pops birthday today."

June 4. Clay Pidgeon. Letter #26. "Briefed at 08:00. Went to point on French Coast just four miles below Boulogne. Two battalions of german troops stationed there. Bombed PFF. Most bombs went in Channel, but some fell on target. 12- 500 lbs. bombs- 1700 gals. gas. Lasted four hours. Bombed from 24,000 ft. About 10 rocket bombs and two burst flak. Easy mission. No fighters of any sort. Wrote letter. To bed."

June 5. Clay Pidgeon. Letter #15 to folks. Letter #27 to Helen. "Ground school and Link Trainer. Went to movie-"My Favorite Blonde." Wrote letters, & to bed."

June 6. <u>"D-DAY</u>" Clay Pidgeon. "Up at 23:45. Didn't even get to sleep. Went on mission to Anselles-Sur-Mer, on French Coast. Bombed gun emplacements, troops, etc. Carried 38- 100 lbs. demolition bombs. 1700 gals. fuel. Bombed from 16,000'. Invasion began at 07:25. Zero hour was 07:30. Our group put up 42 ships in first wave, and 12 in second. 1,350 heavy bombers were in the first wave, & 550 in second. 11,000 planes will be over coast during day. Some Blitz. We bombed PFF- 'Gee Box.' Mission lasted 4 ½ hours. We are alerted again. Up at 15:00. Went to Thury-Harcourt, Coast of France. Bombed in front of our landing troops. Bombed an important road junction. Dropped 12- 500 lbs. bombs. Just group leader (PFF) and us went in alone. Rest of formation didn't find us. Lots of clouds. Good ringside seat up there. Ships and boats of all kinds. Men on beach. Fire and hell all over coast. Bombed from 17,000'. Mission 4 ½ hours. Landed 22:45. Plenty tired."

June 7. Clay Pidgeon. Letter #28 to Helen. "Up at 11:30. Went to lunch and combat meeting. Ground school all afternoon. Supper and a beer with Tunstall. Met Rahn- copilot from Andalusia, Penna. Wrote letters , & to bed. Have 11 missions now."

June 8. Clay Pidgeon. Letter #16 to folks. Letter #29 to Helen. "Up at 08:00. Fresh fried eggs. 10/dozen. Ground school. Nothing new. To bed."

June 9. Clay Pidgeon. "Up at 08:00. Ground school. Received package from Mother. To bed."

June 10. Clay Pidgeon. "Up at 08:00. Ground school. Nothing new. To bed."

June 11. Clay Pidgeon. Letter #30 to Helen. "Up at 03:15. Wanted me to fly, but changed their minds when I got down there. Back to bed. Up at 11:00. Ate lunch. Played cards all afternoon. Won 15 L (pounds sterling). Married six months today. Letter to Helen, and to bed."

June 12. Clay Pidgeon. Letter #17 to folks. "Flew as spare today to Lille-Vondeville, an airfield about 3 miles south of Lille, France. Up at 01:15. We didn't get to go. They blew the place up properly. Our squadron, flying as low groups, blew up the hangars. Good job. Slept all afternoon. Wrote letters, & to bed."

June 13. Clay Pidgeons. Letter #31 to Helen. "Up at 00:30 for mission to Hamburg. Mission scrubbed at 01:00. Back to bed, & up again at 09:00 for combat meeting. Ground school, and at 11:00 I passed out. Just stomach upset. Slept all afternoon, and in good shape again. Wrote letter, & to bed."

June 14. Clay Pidgeons. "Happy Birthday! 23 yrs.- feel older. Grounded today. Link Trainer morning & afternoon. Tired as usual-to bed. Pictures taken at Link Trainer Dept."

June 15. Clay Pidgeon. "Up at 00:30. Took off at 04:30- went to Nantes, Fr. Bombed railroad bridge over river there. Blew it all to Hell. Not too much flak. Tracked us all the way across Nantes. Landed at 12:00. Slept until 17:00, then went to officer's party at Gayhurst Manor, Nr. Newport Paquell. Big old country estate. To bed late."

June 16. Clay Pidgeon. Letter #32 to Helen. Letter #18 to folks. "Up at 09:00. Whole barracks late for Ground school all day. Col. Williams chewed whole squadron out on military courtesy laxity. Wrote letters & to bed."

June 17. Clay Pidgeons. "Up at 01:00. Briefed for mission to Paris. Mission scrubbed at 04:00. Back to bed. Up again at 08:00. Briefed on mission to Orleans, France. Mission all screwed up. Finally bombed bridge over rivers near LeMans, France. Mission lasted six hours. Dingman went down over French coast. Six chutes were seen come out. Also Pederson went down on way back. All chutes came out of his plane. #312 & #163. Now to bed."

June 18. Clay Pidgeon. "Up at 01:00. Went to Hamburg, Germany. Took off at 05:00. Landed at 12:15. It was PFF. Lots of flak at Hamburg. Leader's bombs would not drop. We did not bomb therefore. Went to bed at 14:00. Up for supper.Shower & shave, and to bed again. The other two groups dropped their bombs, and had good results. Right in center of town. 25,500", 100 lb. demolition bombs. (38)"

June 19. Clay Pidgeon. Letter #33 to Helen. Letter #34 to Helen. "Up at 04:00. Briefed for mission to Noball (Pas de Calais) target. "Robot" installations. Mission lasted five hours. 25,000". 38- 100 lb. demos. Did not drop bombs. Clouds 10/10 cover. Interrogated & ate. Then in sack. Wrote letters, & to bed. Moved into Clements room tonight. Nice & private & quiet. "The Chamber." "

June 20. Clay Pidgeon. Letter #19 to folks. "Up at 01:00. Waked up too late for briefing. Took off at 04:30. Went to Hamburg, Germany. Mission lasted 7 ½ hours. 25,000' - 12- 500 lb. bombs. (demos). Bombed oil refineries and docks on south side of river. We flew #4 in lead sqdn. & lead group. After seeing the results, I would say offhand that Hamburg 'has had it.' Just a rubble in the town, anyway. Columns of smoke 20,000' high. The whole river ablaze. Never saw anything like it. An excellent job. Flak heavy-plenty close hits- but none hit us. Some shot up badly. 423rd lost two ships over target. Saw two F.W. 190s. Home and hit the sack. Now have fire going in chamber- Smoking pipe-soon to bed. 16 missions now."

June 21. Clay Pidgeons. "Up at 24:00- in fact, I wasn't in bed yet. Went to Berlin today. Took off at 04:30. Mission lasted 10:50. A long haul. Intense contrails-formation scattered. Flak heavy but widely dispersed. Few enemy fighters. Many fires in Berlin- not much but a rubble now. 1500 Forts & Libs over it today. About 25 Combat Wings. Lancasters (900 of them) were supposed to follow us- but screwed up I guess. Many ships in trouble- ditching, etc. Not as bad as my first one, however. To bed. Need lots of rest. 17 missions now. I was pro-rated 3 missions- have to do 32 missions in my tour now."

June 22. Clay Pidgeons. "Up at 11:30. Briefing at 14:30. Went to Ghent, Belgium. Bombed marshalling yard. We did a perfect job. Hit the M.P.I. right on the nose. No bombs hit the town, only a few yards away. Good formation all the way. Mission lasted about 4 ½ hours. To bed."

June 23. Clay Pidgeons. Letter #20 to folks. Letter #35 to Helen. "Up at 11:30. Briefed for target-Lille, France. Oil tanks. Mission scrubbed at "engine time". Had eggs and toast in "The Chamber" tonight. Staying up to write letters. Sent money-order in folks' letter for $100.xx."

June 24. Clay Pidgeons. "Went to Bremen today. Lots of flak over the target, but the Jerries screwed up. 10/10 overcast. They threw up their barrage too late. We turned right away from it. No flak holes. Rough in the E.T.O. without sleep."

June 25. Clay Pidgeons. "Up at 11:30. Briefed at 14:30. Went to railroad bridge over river near Joigny, France. Did an excellent job of bombing. Bridge should be in the river. A few bombs dropped "over" and went into the marshalling yard. Got back to the chamber at 24:00. Built fire and intended to write letters, but at 24:30 C.Q. came in and said breakfast at 01:00. No sleep again."

June 26. Clay Pidgeon. Letter #36 to Helen. Letter #21 to folks. "Breakfast at 01:00. Briefed for target Munich- secondary Ludwigshaven. A rough trip. Always hit by fighters down there. However, mission scrubbed at taxi time. Back to the sack. Weather too bad. I was going with Speelman. Our crew was not flying. Up again at 11:30. Lunch then took equipment out of ship (#133- Pretty Baby). Free for the rest of the day. Received citation and award of the "Air Medal" today. Citation dated 31st May, 1944."

June 27. Clay Pidgeon. "Up at 09:00. Late for meeting. Went out and shot landings with Malsom. Then went to London in the afternoon."

June 28. "On pass in London."

June 29. "On pass in London. Saw ruins caused by "Doodlebugs." Saw three "bugs" myself. Fascinating things! Got back to the "Senate Chamber" 24:15. Lots of mail awaiting my arrival."

June 30. Clay Pidgeons. Letter #37 to Helen. Letter #22 to folks. "Up at 08:15. Combat meeting. Ground school. Slept all afternoon. Supposed to shoot landings tonight, but didn't receive word. A "booby trap" bomb went off here today. Blew up an airplane. Rocked the whole field. Wrote letters & to bed."

July 1. Clay Pidgeons. Letter #38 to Helen. "Up at 08:15. Missed breakfast again. Combat meeting-ground school-lunch. Nothing all afternoon. Slept. Supper. Shower, shave, feel good. Wrote letter. To bed."

July 2. Clay Pidgeons. Letter #39 to Helen. "Up at 11:30. Practice mission from 14:00 to 17:00. Flew as first-pilot. Peters was co-pilot. Flew #2 in formation. Mac led formation. Pretty good formation today. I'll probably be checked out soon. Wrote letter & to bed."

July 3. Clay Pidgeons. Letter #40 to Helen. "Up at 08:15. Combat meeting- ground school- checked guns and ship. #053 is mine at present. Meeting at 13:15 in "B" mess pertaining to remodeling of officer's club. Should be nice when finished. Ground school all afternoon. Phil Griswold from Oregon left today for home. Probably a big mission tomorrow. To bed. Had toast & butter here in "The Chamber" before Carter & Ristuccia brought it over."

July 4. Clay Pidgeons. Letter #41 to Helen. "Up at 11:30. Meeting at 13:15. Flew two hours transition with Raster. Shot two landings, stalls, turns, etc."

July 5. Clay Pidgeons. "Up at 08:00. Nothing all day. Slept."

July 6. Clay Pidgeons. "Up at 08:00. Combat meeting, etc. Flew in formation over field as Royal Family & Doolittle were here at Princess's christening of the "Rose of York." Mac was co-pilot. Raster pilot. Raster received captain's bars today also. Went with Malsom's crew tonight to Red Cross Aeroclub for dinner. Very nice. Toast & butter with Carter & Shaw, and to bed. Malan was hit in forearm today by .50 cal. Bullet. Over at Dittingdon now in hospital."

July 7. Clay Pidgeons. Letter #23 to folks. "Up at 09:00. Combat meeting. Link Trainer 11-12. Gave operator a lesson (Novinsky). Flew transition 01:40 with Raster. 5 landings. Did O.K. Few beers at club, wrote letters, and in the sack."

July 8. Clay Pidgeons. F.P. Letter #42 to Helen. Letter #43 to Helen. "Up at 08:00. Flew with Raster. Took some Engineers around countryside to take pictures. They took some pictures of Belvoir Castle, the castle that their insignia is copied from. Also Fort Belvoir in the states named after it. Did some good buzzing- 200'. Flew practice gunnery mission in afternoon, but 5 min. after takeoff it was scrubbed. This was my first ride as actual first-pilot. Prokop- new one- was co-pilot. Crunican, Carter, went along. Slept from 17:00 to 21:00. Went over to party at "B" mess. Not many there. Had couple dances with a Red Cross girl, couple beers, and home to bed."

July 9. Clay Pidgeons. Letter #24 to folks. "Up at 08:00. Had breakfast for a change. Supposed to fly X-country in "Pretty Baby", but weather moved in, so all flying was scrubbed. Drank beer all evening, and to bed."

July 10. Clay Pidgeons. Letter #44 to Helen. "Up at 08:15. No breakfast as usual. Practice formation- but #729 had leaking gas tank, so I didn't fly. Flew locally this afternoon for 2 hours. Wrote letter & to bed."

July 11. Clay Pidgeons. "Up at 08:15. Flew 2:30 practice formation in the morning- #065. And 4:00 of the same thing in the afternoon. Maj. Fuhrmeister & Col. Williams met me after I landed- said I did a good job of flying "in the hole", then presented me with a silver bar. Sweated it out for quite a while. Ronczy was flying with me, and he got his too. Carter asked for my gold bar, so I gave it to him. In bed early for a change."

July 12. Clay Pidgeons. Letter #45 to Helen. Letter #25 to folks. "Up at 08:15. Flew 1:05 practice formation today. Briefed for a mission to a "flying bomb site" this afternoon, but mission scrubbed just before station-time. Came back and hit the sack until 18:30- ate supper- showered & shaved- wrote letters- & to bed."

July 13. Clay Pidgeons. Letter #46 to Helen. "Up at 08:15. Cleaned ship #053- 1:00 of Link Trainer, and that was all for the day. Went to movies, saw "Slightly Dangerous". Very poor. Wrote letter, and hit the sack. Got my Special Orders for promotion today. (#180.) 6 July. Effective 27 June."

July 14. Clay Pidgeons. "Up at 08:15. Clean ships in morning. Flew practice formation in afternoon. Glenn Miller & his band were here tonight in celebration of our 200th mission. Miller came & Miller went, & Sage & Crunican slept on- and to bed."

July 15. Clay Pidgeons. Letter #47 to Helen. "Up at 08:15. Went to Dittingdon to see Malan. Looks pretty good. Flew practice formation 4:00 this afternoon. A beautiful formation. A whole wing from our field. Flew Deputy Lead in low group. Supper- a few drinks- wrote letter & to bed."

July 16. Clay Pidgeons. Letter #26 to folks. Letter #48 to Helen. "Up at 03:15 to fly in Wegener's place. He came in drunk. But Allen flew instead and he aborted. Nothing all day- letters & to bed. Received package from home- sandals & cigars."

July 17. Clay Pidgeons. Letter #49 to Helen. "Up at 02:00. Went on my first (F.C.M.) mission as first-pilot. Crunican, Carter, Ristuccia, & Shaw from my regular crew. Good mission. #053. Bombed bridge over canal- hit it on the nose. Bridge near Ham, France. Sleep! Flew #5 in high squadron."

July 18. Clay Pidgeons. "Up at 01:00. Went to Peenemunde, Germany. Bombed rocket manufacturing installation. Hit target on the button. Not too much flak at target (9:30). Long haul. Flew #715-V. beautiful ship. Flew #5 in high squadron. Low airspeed. Stalling out constantly. Crunican, Carter, & Shaw. Good mission. Landed with 500 gal. gas. We carried "Nickel". 10 more missions."

July 19. Clay Pidgeons. "Up at 08:00. Had breakfast for a change. Flew practice formation in the "hole". Beautiful formation. Couris leading. Cleaned ship, shot skeet, & went to squadron meeting. Col. Williams being replaced by Maj. Flanaghan. A good man, I think. Was operations Officer of 369th."

July 20. Clay Pidgeons. "Up at 02:00. Went to Koethen, Germany. Supposed to bomb aircraft-engine factory. Don't know whether we hit it or not. 08:25, #715- Carter & Shaw. Good formation. Flew #3 on group leader (Kesling & Couris). Lots of flak in target area. Some shot up- two wounded men. We got no holes. Exhausted!"

July 21. Clay Pidgeons. Letter #27 to folks. Letter #50 to Helen. "Up at 11:00. Ground school & cleaned ship- #053. Played cards- wrote letters & to bed. Crunican flying in deputy lead today to Schweinfurt. PFF aborted- & Crunican led the wing. Good boy!"

July 22. Clay Pidgeons. Letter #51 to Helen. Letter #28 to folks. "Up at 08:00. Combat meeting. Ground school. Cleaned #053. In afternoon was assigned #715 at last. We cleaned her up good, and decided to name her 'Pleasure Bent'. Good, appropriate name. We'll get her painted up real soon. Played cards, wrote letters, & to bed." (crossed out: "Wrote in for pictures of Princess. Three sets.")

July 23. Clay Pidgeon. Letter #52 to Helen. Letter #29 to folks. "Up at 11:00. Flew solo cross-country to mt. Farm, High Wickham (SHAEF), Cambridge, Oxford, Peterborough, & return. #715 a beauty. "Pleasure Bent". Wrote letters, shower & shave, & bed. PFF just landed. Everyone restricted tonight. Maybe something cooking."

July 24. Clay Pidgeons. "Up at 02:00. Went on mission to the Normandy front. Bombed troops, etc. Just like D-Day. Bombed from 15,000'. Visibility poor, but good results were obtained. Would hate to have been down there. We dropped 38- 100# bombs-demos. Little flak- good mission. Pleasure Bent has scavenger- pump trouble in #1, so we had to take #065. Rough!"

July 25. Clay Pidgeons. Letter #53 to Helen. Letter #30 to folks. "Up at 02:00. Went on same mission as yesterday. Bombed the same places. The whole 8th A.F. out again. Also Ninth A.F. with mediums & fighter-bombers. Little flak again. Bombed from 12,000'. Sitting ducks. Pleasure Bent in rare form. Painted "Emily" on fuselage this afternoon, & Carter painted "Florence". To bed."

July 26. Clay Pidgeons. "Up at 08:00. Practice formation. Pass started at noon. Carter & I worked on ship. I painted Helen on left of cockpit. Carter painted Carol – Don on turret. Went to bed early."

July 27. Leicester. "Up at 11:00. Ate, showered, & shaved, and off to Leicester on train. Went to Grand Hotel- sent me to Mrs. Wandle's- #41 New Walk. Nice boarding house. Nice town."

July 28. Leicester. "Fresh eggs & ham & toast & butter for breakfast- also the inevitable 'tea'. Met G.I.'s. Home at 23:30. Big party in my room. Smashed chairs & to bed. Good 2-day pass. Road (sic) horseback for 1 ½ hours. With Australian para-trooper."

July 29. Clay Pidgeons. Letter #54 to Helen. Letter #31 to folks. "Up at 08:00. Combat meeting. Cleaned ship & talked with crew on interphone discipline, etc. Lunch & combat meeting again. Practice formation, but my ship was 'out', so I didn't have to fly. Good pictures from home today. Wrote letters & to bed."

July 30. Clay Pidgeons. "Up at 11:30. Chow, and then practice formation in afternoon. Flew with Fell*, leading high squadron. Good position. Played cards & to bed. *he as co-pilot."

July 31. Clay Pidgeons. Letter #55 to Helen. Letter #32 to folks. "Up at 04:30. Went to Munich. Led high squadron in low group. Did fairly well for first time. Flak accurate tracking type. Our wing - #306th- led 8th A.F. today. Gen. Turner went in lead ship. Deputy had to take over on bomb run- Tell. 09:40- long mission. Co-pilot was Fowler- 1000 flying hours. His first mission. Six more. Wrote letters, & to bed."

August 1. Clay Pidgeons. "Up at 08:00. Combat meeting. Got ready & left on flak leave to rest home - Stanbridge Earls, Romsey, Hants. Arrived at rest home 22:00. Hot chocolate, & to bed. Beautiful place."

August 2. Stanbridge Earls, Romsey, Hants. "(Seven miles N.E. of Southampton)."

August 3, 4, 5. Writing crossed out.

August 6, 7. Blank.

August 8. Clay Pidgeons. "Arrived here at 20:00. Unpacked, talked with boys, & to bed."

August 9. Clay Pidgeons. "Up at 08:00. Combat meeting, etc. Flew to Tangmere, R.A.F., to get #611 that McNeil had landed there from mission day before. Flew target ship. Good lunch. Saw "Lucky Milan" there- English fighter ace. Boys went to Munich. Plumb flew my ship- came back with no fin or rudder. Cardon in #063 chewed it off in formation. Went to movies- saw "Algiers", & to bed. Sent cablegrams to folks & Helen."

August 10. Clay Pidgeons. Letter #33 to folks. Letter #34 to folks. Letter #56 to Helen. Letter #57 to Helen. "Up at 11:30. Mission scheduled. I was to lead high squadron, but it was scrubbed. Wrote letters, & to bed. Sent two money orders home- $100 each in letters #33 & #34 to folks."

August 11. Clay Pidgeons. Letter #58 to Helen. Letter #35 to folks. "Up at 08:00. Combat meeting. Practice formation from 10:00 til 14:30. I led low squadron. Good formation. Shot two target off target- ship. Flew in #099. Saw movie "Calling Dr. Gillespie", with Lionel Barrymore. Played cards with enlisted men, wrote letters, & to bed."

August 12. Clay Pidgeons. "Up at 02:30. Bombed air strip about 20 miles N.E. of Paris. Led low squadron in lead group. No flak near us. Carried 38- 100 lb. demolition bombs. Some carried frogs (frags?) Good mission. To bed early."

August 13. Clay Pidgeons. Letter #59 to Helen. Letter #36 to folks. "Up at 06:30. Bombed road on west side of Seine River west of Paris, to help trap 30 German divisions expected to retreat across Seine. Lots of accurate flak, but we got none in high sqdn. I led high sqdn. Saw 3 ships go down. Pretty good mission. Carried 38- 100 lb. demos. Bombardier, Gruenig, had to chop one out that hung up. Wrote letters, & to bed."

August 14. Clay Pidgeons. Letter #60 to Helen. "Up at 08:15. Meeting. Saw propaganda movie on Anglo-American relationship. Slept all afternoon. Feel pretty old these days. Plenty tired."

August 15. Clay Pidgeons. Letter #61 to Helen. Letter #37 to folks. "Up at 07:25 because of explosion of #558- 369th Sqdn. Terrible accident. 5 killed. Nothing to do all day. Letters & to bed."

August 16. Clay Pidgeons. Letter #62 to Helen. Letter #38 to folks. "Very little doing today. Up at 09:00. Got haircut, etc. Saw "Guadacanal Diary" tonight. Wrote letters, & to bed. The boys went to Leipzig today. All planes in for repairs. Quite a bit of flak."

August 17. Clay Pidgeons. Letter #63 to Helen. Letter #39 to folks. "Up at 08:15. Ground school, etc. Flew #063- ferried it over to Alconbury sub-depot this afternoon. Letters, & to bed. Received another Oak leaf Cluster today."

August 18. Clay Pidgeons. "Up at 08:30. Supposed to slow-time #133, but #2 engine had bad mags. Went to movies- "The Great Man's Lady"- with Charles Capaldi (High school friend) from Fkd.- and to bed."

August 19. Clay Pidgeons. Letter #64 to Helen. Letter #40 to folks. "Up at 08:00. Ground school, & sack time. Magee & Hanson are back. Saw "Road Agent". Letters, & to bed."

August 20. Clay Pidgeons. "Up at 08:15. Ground school, etc. Very bad weather. To bed."

August 21. Clay Pidgeons. "Up at 08:15. Ground school, etc. Still closed in. To bed."

August 22. Clay Pidgeons. Letter #65 to Helen. Letter #41 to folks. "Up at 08:15. Ground school again. Saw movie "Crystal Ball". Ceiling zero. To bed."

August 23. Clay Pidgeons. "Up at 08:15. Ground school, etc. to bed."

August 24. Clay Pidgeons. "Flew mission to Merseburg area. Bombed Lutzkendorf. Intense heavy flak at target. Long haul. 10- 500# demos. Led high sqdn.- lead group. In the sack. (Last mission- 30!)"

August 25. Clay Pidgeons. "Up at 08:15. Ground school, etc. Saw "The Song of Burnadette." Very good. To bed. Checked Fowler out today."

August 26. Clay Pidgeons. Letter #66 to Helen. Letter #42 to folks. "Up at 08:15. Going on pass today."

August 27. "On pass."

August 28. Clay Pidgeons. Letter #67 to Helen. Letter #42 to folks. "Had a good pass, except for news of Steve. His #18 mission. Cambridge University doesn't compare to our college campuses, etc. However, buildings are very old & beautiful. King's Chapel is very beautiful. Val Otterson & Manuel are supposed to have gone down. Ramlow is in Sweden. Letters & to bed."

August 29. "In hospital on a little rest cure."

August 30. "Still resting."

August 31. "Still resting in peace."

September 1. Clay Pigeons. Letter #68 to Helen. Letter #43 to folks. "Kicked out of hospital today. Also taken off combat. Going home they say. Wonderful. Sent cablegram. Also money order in folks' letter #43. Letters & to bed."

September 2. Clay Pigeons. Letter #69 to Helen. Letter #44 to folks. "Up at 11:30. Great to be a kiwi-paddlefoot or groundgripper. Letter & bed."

September 3. Clay Pigeons. "Up at noon. Slept."

September 4. Clay Pigeons. "Up at noon. Non-combat man now. Great life. Still raining. Slept. Saw "Two Girls & a Sailor." Very good show."

September 5. Clay Pigeons. Letter #70 Helen. Letter #45 folks. "Up at noon. Played "Hearts" with crew. Wrote letters & to bed."

September 6. Clay Pigeons. Letter #71 Helen. Letter #46 folks. "Up at noon. Played cards. Slept. Missed supper. Letters & to bed."

September 7. Clay Pigeons. Letter #72 Helen. "Up at noon. Read articles in Reader's Digest. Letter. Clements just came in. Great to see him again. To bed."

September 8-29. Blank pages.

September 30. "Mailed $100.xx money orders, each, to Dad & Helen."

The diary ends here, except for the list of missions at the end, #1- 29.

Footnotes to Diary (Chapter 3)

All missions cited in the diary are described in detail in Appendices B, C, and D. Named individuals are identified upon their first citation, and are thereafter referenced by that citation date. B-17s are likewise identified by serial number and other data upon their first citation, and subsequently referenced by that date. Identification of individuals was based on their overlap with RCS's tour in the 367th B.S.; most were pilots or co-pilots in this squadron.

April 2

Kearney A.A.F. – Military airport located near Kearney, Buffalo County, Nebraska. Kearney Army Airfield construction was completed in February, 1943; it served as both a training and a processing base. By 1944, bombardment processing units for B-17 crews and aircraft were stationed there.

Ellie – also called "Helen," was RCS's wife and the author's mother.

April 4

Dow Field – Dow Army Field (1942) served as a point of embarkation for aircraft bound for Europe via the Great Circle Route. The base later became part of the Strategic Air Command and was closed officially in 1968.

April 5

Folks – Harry Ransley Sage (father) and Emily G. Moleton Sage (mother).

April 6

Nielsen – William R. Neilson (367th B.S.), or Harvey C. Nielsen (365th B.S.)
Reynolds – John L. Reynolds (368th B.S.). Deceased.
Carlson –Norman P. Carlson (369th B.S.).
Lauer – S/SGT. F.B. (Fred) Lauer, tail gunner in RCS's crew (page 68).
Crunican – 2nd Lt. C.J. (Charles) Crunican, bombardier, in RCS's crew (page 68). Tour.

April 8

Goose Bay – in 1941, Canada built this air base (RCAF Station Goose Bay) and allowed the USAAF to build its own facilities there).
Ronny – not identified.
Chuck – Charles Crunican (April 6).

April 9

Meeks Field, Kaflavik (sic), Iceland – bomber field, dedicated in March, 1943, and used as a stopover point for USAAF transatlantic military flights. Keflavik is located on the Reykjanes peninsula on the southwest portion of the island.
Basset Hound – British tanker, no further information.

April 11

Nutts Corner- AAF-235, R.A.F. station near Belfast, Ireland, used also as a hub for U.S. aircraft en route to Europe.
B-24 Liberators (120 Sqdn.) used this base for maritime patrols.
Dingy-Dingy I – no information.
R.A.F. – Royal Air Force.

April 12

W.A.A.F. – Women's Auxiliary Air Force.

April 13

Blanks (destination points) – not filled in.

April 14

Beattie Hall (sic) – Beatty Hall, Stone, Berkshire, AAF 518. 8th A.F. Service Comd.

April 15

Chuck- (April 6)
Women's Land Army – active in WWI and re-formed in 1939 in the U.K. Women worked on farms and in factories to support the war effort.

April 17

Peters- Frank J. (368th B.S.), Lucien F. (369th B.S.), or Sanford (423rd B.S.) Peters
Sandlin- not listed in 306th B.G.
Cusick- not listed in 306th B.G.
Mehmer-not listed in 306th B.G. Note: These last 3 men might have been assigned to another Group at this time.

April 18

Mac – most likely 2nd Lt. Talmadge G. McDonough, pilot; flew two missions #099-S/PFF, HIGH on D-Day (see Appendices C and D). Tour. A photograph of this crew, with co-pilot RCS, is shown on page 87.

April 19

Bovingdon – town in Hertfordshire, England, site of the 8th A.F. (1942-1946) and post-war R.A.F. airfield.

April 20

I.P. – Initial Point of Bomb Run
Joe Tunstall- listed as 369th B.S., and not 308th as stated in diary. Deceased.
Mac (April 18)
91st, 306th, 92nd Groups – Heavy Bombardment Groups of the 8th A.F.. The 91st was stationed at Bassingbourne (AF121) (1942-1945). 306th (see Introduction). 92nd (1942-1945, inactivated in France 1946).

April 23

Chuck, Mac, and Sandy – Crunican (April 6), McDonough (April 18) and unidentified, possibly Sandlin (April 17).

April 24

Ross's Group (389th) – Heavy Bombardment Group (Dec. 1942 – Sept. 1945), saw action during Normandy invasion and Battle of the Bulge (stationed at this time at Hethel, England).

April 27

Mac (April 18).

April 28

Thurleigh – AAF 111, 306th B.G., 367th B.S. (see Introduction).

April 29

Clay Pidgeon (sic) – despite otherwise near-perfect spelling, grammar, and punctuation, RCS consistently misspelled "Pigeon" as "Pidgeon" throughout the diary, until September 1.

67th – 67th Bombardment Squadron, 44th B.G. (Heavy) (1941-1946), 8th A.F.

May 2

Tunstall (April 20)

May 3

Mac (April 18)

May 4

"Slim" Somerville – Richard J. Somerville, pilot. Tour (25 missions).

May 5

Matichka- Louis F. Matichka, pilot. MIA (Missing in Action)/POW (Prisoner of War).

Col. Raper-William S. Raper, C.O. 367th B.S. (March 6, 1943-August 18, 1943) (see page 88, top).

May 7

Chuck & Mac – (April 6 and April 18).

Flak – aircraft defense cannon (Fliegenabwehrkanone), anti-aircraft artillery (Germany).

Mrs. Ross – wife or mother of Ross (April 24)?

May 8

PFF – Pathfinder, a type of radar (H2x) used to locate targets (Westgate, p. 24).

May 10
Tunstall (April 20).

May 11
#053- 42-40053 "Prayers & Patches", G, arrived 1/11/44, departed 4/10/44.

May 12
#729- 42-30729, F, arrived 5/2/44, salvaged 5/29/44.
Ristuccia – Sgt. Lawrence A. (Larry) Ristuccia, Jr., left waist gunner, in RCS's crew (page 68).
Dickhaus – S/SGT. Edward F. (Dick) Dickhaus, right waist gunner, in RCS's crew (page 68). Deceased.

May 13 (see Appendix D for this date)
#278- 42-97278 Del Cheyenne 12/2/44; Rapid City 4/3/44; Gr Island 19/4/44;Ass 398BG Nuthampstead 25/4/44; no ops, tran 367BS/306BG (GY-K) Thurleigh 12/5/44; MIA Ruhland 12/9/44 w Chas Wagener, Bill Griffin, Don Marsh, Bill Stewart, Joe Stroyoff, Jack Krahn, John Eden (7POW); Bill Gardiner, Henry Rodgers (KIA - Killed in Action); e/a, cr Uedersee, Ger; MACR 8833. UMBRIAGO. Note that this ship was transferred to the 367th and went down on September 12, 1944. MACR is the official report of the MIAs.
Rentschler – Mr. Rentschler was vice-president of Mutual Rendering Co., Philadelphia, at this time (Chapter 1).

May 14
#065-42-31065, G, arrived 10/19/43, MIA Ruhland (w. Bailey).

May 16
Parnes – 2nd Lt. Arnold J. Parnes, bombardier (367th B.S.). KIA April 11, 1944. (*Combat Chronology Supplement*, p.206; Losses of the 8th & 9th Air Forces, Vol.3, p.642).
Peters, Maxwell Field – Montgomery, Alabama. No further information.

May 18
Ryan – possibly Steve Ryan (August 28). 385th B.S., went down July 12, 1944.

May 19
Ronczy – 2nd Lt. Edward L. (Ed) Ronczy, navigator, in RCS's crew (p 68). Tour.
Bill Grey – not identified.
Mrs. Platt – not identified.

May 21
Pancrast (sic) – St. Pancras, Railway Station, Central London terminus.

May 22
#063- 42-107063, G, arrived 5/18/44, salvaged 12/3/44.

May 23
Allen – William R. Allen, pilot, flew #198-D HIGH on D-Day (see Appendix D). Tour.
Crunican- (April 6)

May 30
Malsom – Ralph B. Malsom, pilot (367th B.S.). Tour. (July 6).

Summary of 367th B.S. activity in May 1944. Lt. Col. Robert C. Williams, C.O. The squadron flew more missions than in any other month since its inception. Of the 20 missions flown by the 306th B.G., the 367th participated in 18 (previously, the highest number was 16). Lt. Edward D. Magee received the DFC, and Captain Fuhrmeister was promoted to Major. Lt. Daniel L. Speelman was promoted from 2nd to 1st Lt.

June 2
Mac – (April 18).

June 3
Dingman – 1st Lt. Virgil W. Dingman, pilot (367th B.S.), flew #312-T LEAD on D-Day (see Appendix D). (June 17). EVADEE.

June 6 (see Appendices C and D)
"Gee-Box" – a reference to Gee-H radar bombing technique, usually with PFF.
"Went in alone" – See Appendices C & D for this date. The page in the diary describing this event is shown on page 89.

June 7
Rahn – Marshall J. Rahn, copilot (367th B.S.). Tour.

June 14
These photos are shown on pages 79 through 81.

June 16
Col. Williams – Robert C. Williams, C.O., 367th B.S., May 3, 1944-July 18, 1944.

June 17
Dingman – (June 3). Crashed at Bacqueville on June 17, 1944 in B-17 #42-97312, POW.
Peterson – Joseph W. Pedersen, pilot (367th B.S.), flew #278-K LEAD on D-Day (see Appendix C). Crashed near LeMans on June 17, 1944 in B-17 #42-38163, MIA/POW.
Note: Peterson in #143 also flew in that mission, but there is no record of this pilot in the 367th B.S. A Walter R. Peterson, pilot (367th B.S.) was KIA on April 24, 1944.
#312- 42-97312, G, arrived 5/12/44, MIA Noyen (w. Dingman).
#163- 42-38163, G, arrived 2/29/44, 6/17/44 MIA Noyen (w. Pedersen)

June 19
Clements – George W. Clements, 367th B.S. EVADEE.

June 20 (see Appendix D)
423rd - Bombardment Squadron (Heavy), deployed to England in September, 1942, inactivated in December, 1946. Highly decorated for service in Europe during WWII.
F.W. 190s – Focke-Wulf 190 (German interceptor fighter).

June 21 (see Appendix C)
Forts – Flying Fortresses (B-17s).
Libs – Consolidated B-24 Liberators (heavy bombers).
Lancasters – British Avro Lancasters (heavy bombers). Note: See Appendices C & D for this date.

June 22
M.P.I. – Main Point of Bomb Impact.

June 24
E.T.O. – European Theater of Operations.

June 25 (see Appendix D)

June 26
Speelman – Daniel L. Speelman, pilot & co-pilot (367th B.S.). Tour.
#133 – Pretty Baby – 42-97133 (page 68).
42-97133 Del Cheyenne 29/1/44; Kearney 12/2/44; Presque Is 2/3/44; Ass 367BS/306BG Thurleigh 26/3/44; tran 91BG 30/5/45; 105m, Ret US Bradley 11/6/45; 4168 BU Sth Plains 21/10/45; RFC Kingman 8/12/45. PRETTY BABY.

June 27
Malsom – (May 30).

June 29
"Doodlebugs" – V-1 flying bomb, a German jet-propelled bomb that caused substantial damage, especially to London.

June 30
"Booby trap" bomb. Blew up an airplane....No record found of this incident.
Summary of 367th B.S. activity in June, 1944. Promotions from 2nd to 1st Lt.: Virgil W. Dingman, George W. Clements, William R. Allen, and Talmadge G. McDonough.

July 2
Peters – Ben H. Peters, pilot & co-pilot (same Peters as May 16th?). Tour.
Mac- (April 18)

July 3
#053 – (May 11).
Phil Griswold (Oregon) – Phil G. Griswold, pilot & co-pilot. Tour.
Carter – T/SGT. Donald M. (Don) Carter, top turret gunner and flight engineer, in RCS's crew (page 68). Note: referred to as Radio Operator in June 6, 1944 report (see Appendix D).
Ristuccia – (May 12).
"probably a big mission tomorrow"... There was not.

July 4
Raster – Perry E. Raster, pilot, flew #547 on D-Day (see Appendices C and D, and page 88, bottom). Tour.

July 6
Christening of "Rose of York"/Gen. James Doolittle present. George G. Roberts, Radio Operator (367th B.S., 306th B.G., USAAF) reported that a new B-17G arrived at Thurleigh in March, 1944, and was named by their crew "Princess Elizabeth" (daughter of King George VI and Queen Elizabeth). Because of the possibility of its demise being interpreted as a bad omen, the name was changed to "Rose of York," and the white rose (House of York) was painted on the aircraft. On July 6, 1944, the King, Queen, Princess Elizabeth, and Gen. James Doolittle arrived to christen this ship. Roberts flew his final 16 missions on the "Rose." (www.justinmuseum.com/oralbio/robertsgg.bio). This ship was MIA, Berlin, February 3, 1945. Photographs of this event are shown on pages 90 through 92.
Raster – (July 4)
Mac – (April 18)
Malsom's crew – (June 27)
Carter – (July 3)
Shaw – S/SGT.Ralph W. Shaw, ball turret gunner, in RCS's crew (p 68).
Malan- S/SGT. E.A. (Everett) Malan, top turret gunner, in RCS's crew until wounded.

July 7
Novinsky – radio operator. Milton Novinsky (369th B.S.)?
Raster – (July 4).

July 8
Belvoir Castle – Leicestershire.
Raster – (July 4).
Prokop – Louis P. Prokop, pilot, co-pilot with RCS. Tour. Deceased.
Crunican – (April 6).
Carter – (July 3).

July 9
Pretty Baby – (June 26).

July 10
#729- 42-30729, F, arrived 5/2/44, salvaged 5/29/44. Note: The Squadron Diary mentions Lt. Irving B. Pedersen as pilot on this date.

July 11
#065 – (May 14)
Maj. Fuhrmeister – Dinwiddie Fuhrmeister, U.S.A.A.F., B-17 pilot, Operations Officer, 367th B.S., (25 missions), recipient of D.F.C.
Col. Williams – (June 16).
Ronczy and Carter – (May 19 and July 3, respectively).

July 13
#053 – (May 11)
promotion- to First Lieutenant.

July 14
Glenn Miller – American jazz musician and bandleader, known for his "Big Band" of the swing era (page 93). He disappeared while flying over the English Channel to entertain US troops in France, December 1944. He was 40 years old.
Sage and Crunican – RCS and Chuck (April 6).

July 15
Malan – (July 6).

July 16
Wegener – Charles C. Wegener, pilot, MIA/POW. Deceased.
Allen – (May 23).

July 17 (see Appendix D)
F.C.M. – First Combat Mission (as first pilot).
Crew – Crunican (April 6); Carter (July 3), Ristuccia (May 12), Shaw (July 6).
#053 – (May 11).

July 18
#715-V- 43-37715, G, later named "Lassie Come Home", arrived 6/13/44, departed 1/8/45.
Crunican (April 6), Carter (July 3), and Shaw (July 6)
"Nickel" – propaganda leaflets dropped by air.

July 19
Couris – Joseph Couris, pilot (367th B.S.). Tour.
Maj. Flanaghan/369th – Charles E. Flannagan, 306th B.G., 367th B.S., C.O. July 19, 1944-October 14, 1944, previously Operations Officer of the 369th.Flannagan flew #658 PFF, LEAD, on D-Day (see Appendix D), although this might not be the same man.

July 20
#715 – (July 18)
Carter (July 3) & Shaw (July 6).
Kesling- Earl W. Kesling, Operations Officer, 367th B.S. August 20, 1944 – October 15, 1944; C.O. October 15, 1944 – April 22, 1945. Deceased. (page 93).
Couris – (July 19).

July 21
#053 – (May 11)
#715 – (July 18)

July 23
#715 – (July 18)

July 24 (see Appendices C and D)
#715 – (July 18)
#065 – (May 14). Note: See Appendices C & D for this date and for July 25.

July 25 (see Appendices C and D)
Ninth A.F. – U.S.A.A.F. combat air force that functioned in the European Theater (1943-1945). Also saw action in North Africa (1942).
"Pleasure Bent" – "Emily" (RCS's mother) and "Florence" (possibly Carter's mother?).

July 26
Helen – RCS's wife
Carter – (July 3)
Carol – Don – possibly Don Carter's wife?

July 30
Fell – co-pilot or pilot Tell? (see July 31).

July 31 (see Appendix D)
Gen. Turner – Brigadier General Howard M. Turner, 40th Bombardment Wing (8th A.F. – 1st Bombardment Division, D-Day).
Tell – Charles M. Tell, pilot. Tour.
Fowler – Ward R. Fowler, pilot, co-pilot, in RCS's crew (page 68). Tour.

Summary of 367th B.S. activity in July 1944. On July 18, Flannagan was transferred to the 367th as C.O. Promotions from 1st Lt. to Captain included Henry B. Hanson, Ben H. Peters, Perry E. Raster, and Ralph B. Malsom. Promotions from 2nd to 1st Lt. included Robert C. Sage, Charles Tell, Charles Wegener, Ed Ronczy, Marion C. Plumb, Williams

McNeil, Charles J. Crunican, and Joseph P. Couris. Recipients of the DFC included Lts. Crunican, Speelman, and Marshall J. Rahn.

August 1
Stanbridge (sic) Earls – Standbridge Earls, rest home near Southampton; Hampshire AAF 503 (pages 82-85).

August 9
#611- 42-37611, "Fuddles Folly", arrived 6/12/44, transferred to 381st B.G. in May, 1945.
McNeil – Williams H. McNeil, pilot, flew #042-F, LEAD, on D-Day (see Appendix C). Deceased.
"Lucky Milan" (sic) – Born in South Africa and originally a ship's second officer, Adolph Gysbert "Sailor" Malan was an RAF flying Ace credited with 32 "kills" during WWII (page 94). He was awarded among other honors the DSO (Distinguished Service Order) & Bar and the DFC & Bar. He was C.O. at Biggin Hill in 1943 and of the Advanced Gunnery School Catfoss in 1944 (commencing in July). After his release from the RAF in 1946, he fought against South African Apartheid until his death from Parkinson's Disease in 1963. *The author thanks Jean Prescott (Mighty Eighth Air Force Museum) for this information.*
Plumb – Marion C. Plumb, pilot
Cordon/#063 – Robert L. Cardon, pilot/ship (May 22). Tour.

August 11
#099- 42-32099, G, "Fightin' Carbarn Hammerslaw", arrived 3/12/44, MIA Berlin (w. Manning) 12/5/44.

August 12
Frogs or frags – meaning not clear.

August 13
Gruenig – LTC Robert D. Gruenig, bombardier, in RCS's crew. Tour.

August 15
Explosion of #558 in 369th Squadron – 42-31558 Del Denver 21/11/43; Kearney 14/12/43; Chicago 18/12/43; Syracuse 19/12/43; Presque Is 21/12/43; Ass 369BS/306BG (WW-M) Thurleigh 21/1/44; MIA Erding 24/4/44 w/Gil Vandermarliere, cp-Bill James, n-Ray Uhrich, b-Sid Shertzer, ettg-George Vogt, ro-Willard Elliott, btg-Earl Wynn, wg Jim Copeman, wg-Everett Minto, tg-Walt Lastinger (10POW); e/a, cr Hoerburg, Ger?; MACR 4282. Highly decorated (The Fightin' Bitin') bombardment squadron (heavy), deployed to Thurleigh, England in September, 1942. Note: The Mighty Eighth Air Force Museum Veteran's Database Record lists co-pilot 1st Lt. William R. James (369th B.S.) as shot down 24 April 1944 in B-17 #42-31558, POW.

August 17
#063 – (May 22).

August 18
#133 – (June 26).
Capaldi - Charles B. Capaldi (Philadelphia), 423rd B.S..

August 19
Magee- Edward W. Magee, pilot, co-pilot. 2 Tours.
Hanson- Henry E. Hanson, pilot. 2 Tours.

August 24 (see Appendix C)
Mission #30 ? – 29 missions are listed in the diary (see Appendix B), but RCS could have been referring to 30 as his final mission. See Appendices C & D for this date.

August 25
Fowler - co-pilot, flew twice with RCS (page 68). Also identified on page 68 as "? radio operator and gunner". (July 31).

August 28
Steve – possible reference to Steve Ryan (May 18) (see poem, Chapter 3, page 86, written by Helen Sage). Note: Ryan was not in the 367th B.S.
Val Otterson – 2nd Lt. Val L. Otterson, co-pilot (92nd B.G., 407th B.S.). Shot down into North Sea by flak in B-17 #42-97245 on June 20, 1944. KIA, buried in Cambridge, England. Listed in "Service Personnel Not Recovered following WWII," 6/20/44.

Manuel – 2nd Lt. Charles A. Manuel, co-pilot (385th B.G./548th B.S.). Rammed by enemy aircraft in B-17 #42-31787 and crashed at Langerhain south of Koblenz May 12, 1944. The target was an aircraft repair factory. KIA.

Ramlow -2nd Lt. Charles R. Ramlow, co-pilot (452nd B.G./729th B.S.), shot down in B-17 #42-39930 at Rurrlo, Holland, April 29, 1944. He was lodged at different residences in Holland nearly a year and rejoined Allied Forces on March 10, 1945.

Summary of the 367th B.S. activity in August, 1944. McDonough was promoted from 1st Lt. to Captain. Captain Earl W. Kesling (369th B.S.) was assigned to the 367th on August 19, and was promoted to Squadron Operations Officer on August 20.

September 7

Clements – (June 19).

Notes from Squadron Diary for September, 1944. On September 12 (Ruhland mission), Lt. Charles Wegener went down, with No.3 engine on fire and the tail assembly shot away. Four chutes were seen leaving the a/c (aircraft). On September 17, Lt. Couris (Volkel area) had to land at Lavenham because of battle damage and to hasten the delivery of his wounded waist gunner, S/Sgt. Albert M. Christensen, to a doctor.

DFCs were awarded to McDonough, McNeil, Plumb, Ronczy, Tell, and Wegener. The Purple Heart was awarded to Lt. William R. Allen.

Summary of 367th B.S. activity in October 1944. The DFC was awarded to RCS and to Allen.

"Pretty Baby" and crew. Handwritten by RCS *verso*: "Pretty Baby. Crew: Picture – had just flown a practice formation flight around England—400' altitude! Left to right standing: Charles Crunican Bombardier, Fred Lauer, Tail Gunner, Guess who Pilot,? – co-pilot, Don Carter Top Turret gunner & flight engineer. Kneeling left to right: Ralph Shaw, Ball Turret gunner, Ed Ronczy Navigator, Larry Ristuccia Left Waist gunner, ? Radio operator and gunner (FOWLER)?, Dick Dickhaus, Right waist gunner.
Notes: 1. Radio operator replaced Everett Malan—wounded and in hospital. 2. Co-pilot—flew with me twice—Fowler?—we experienced shortage of personnel from time to time."
This aircraft was likely #42-97133: Del Cheyenne 29/1/44; Kearney 12/2/44; Presque Is 2/3/44; Ass 367BS/306BG Thurleigh 26/3/44; tran 91BG 30/5/45; 105m, RetUS Bradley 11/6/45; 4168 BU S[th] Plains 21/10/45; RFC Kingman 8/12/45. PRETTY BABY. *Information courtesy of Dr. Rogers-Price*. Note that this ship flew 105 missions!

Eighth Air Force B-17s over Europe (note "K" and triangle).

Eighth Air Force B-17s, in formation, over Europe.

A crash landing – "B17 blown up/explos. of Bombs/Crash landing" (*verso*).

RCS in snow – Iceland or Labrador, dated April 8-9 (1944).

RCS bicycling in Stone, England (Beattie Hall), April 16, 1944.

Scenery around Thurleigh, England, c1944. From the collection of Robert G. Shultz. From Hanes City, Florida, Shultz served as a Radio Operator on the B-17 "Maryland, My Maryland". Shultz's crew reached ETO via the southern route, and photographs in this collection include scenes from South America and Africa. The Maryland, My Maryland was assigned to the 306th B.G., 367th B.S., which operated from Thurleigh-Bedford, England. *Courtesy of the Mighty Eighth Air Force Museum Archives, Savannah, Georgia.*

"Seigel, Leahy & Vannucci" (written *verso* in pencil). Edward W. Leahy, deceased. From the collection of Robert G. Shultz. *Courtesy of the Mighty Eighth Air Force Museum.*

RCS, admiring the English countryside, dated May 15, 1944.

RCS in Thurleigh, England, dated May 15, 1944.

"Bob" – a photograph from England, sent by RCS to his mother.

RCS in front of unidentified ship.

RCS (third from *left*) posing with fellow officers of the 367th B.S.

RCS (left) and crew member Don Carter (top turret gunner and flight engineer). Note nose art.

RCS (*left*) and unidentified airman. *Verso*: "Link Trainer – June 14, 1944. Clay Pidgeon Squadron. "To my best girl, Ellie [his wife]".

RCS in cockpit. *Verso:* "Link Trainer – June 14, 1944. Clay Pidgeon Squadron. To my sweet wife." On this date (his birthday) RCS was 23 years old.

RCS, likely the Link Trainer identified on pages 79 and 80.

Standbridge Earls rest home in England, 1944.

Standbridge Earls, also referred to as the "flakhouse."

RCS (*right*) and Don Carter (*left*) at Standbridge Earls rest home; according to the diary this would have been August 29—September 1, 1944.

RCS with golf club, "relaxing" at Standbridge Earls rest home.

Standbridge Earls – handwritten *verso*: "View from my room of rear of English house (three houses in fact)."

Standbridge Earls – handwritten *verso*: "The home of the 'egg girl' – she was lovely! 1944."

Poem to Bo-Bo on
V-J- Day

Tonight, darling, of
you I'm proud,
But I don't feel like
singing loud,
And so from parties
I take my leave,
To thank God for
men like you and
Steve!
Heroes all,
But what for?
There is no war
To end all war!

(over)

I'm not an emotional
cuss,
Why all this fuss?
We've made the world
safe for our son,
Pray God he won't
from an enemy run;
May he be courageous,
strong, a gallant lad,
As fine and clean
as his heroic Dad.

P.S. – I love you, Bobby.

Ellie

Poem written by my mother to my father, scrap 2-3/4" x 4-1/2", and inserted into his diary:

Poem to Bo-Bo on V-J Day (August 15, 1945).
Tonight darling, of you I'm proud,
But I don't feel like singing loud.
And so from parties I take my leave,
To thank God for men like you and Steve!
Heroes all, but what for? There is no war to end all war!
I'm not an emotional cuss, Why all this fuss?
We've made the world safe for our son, Pray God he won't from an enemy run.
May he be courageous, strong, a gallant lad, As fine and clean as his heroic Dad.
P.S. I love you, Bobby. Ellie.

Note: Steve (Ryan) went down on his 18th mission.

Talmadge McDonough Crew. From Strong, Russell A., *Combat Crews*, p. 150.

"Colonel Wm. S. Raper-(former C.O.) Grp. Executive" (written *verso*). From the collection of Robert G. Shultz (see caption to Figure 3-7). *Courtesy of the Mighty Eighth Air Force Museum.*

"Perry E. Raster 2212 N 61st St Wauwatusa, Wisconsin" (written on scrapbook page). From the collection of Robert G. Shultz. *Courtesy of the Mighty Eighth Air Force Museum.*

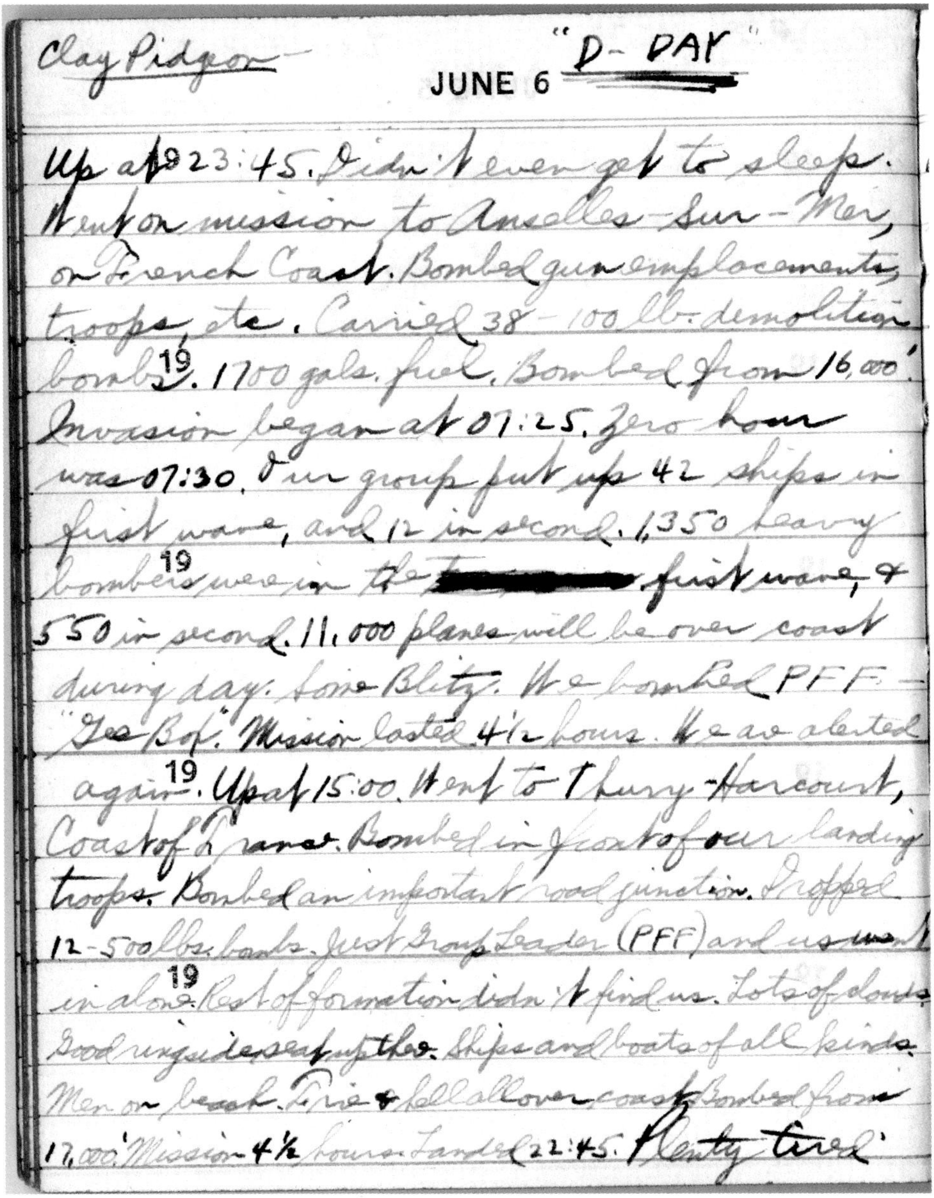

Clay Pidgeon "D-DAY"

JUNE 6

Up at 23:45. Didn't even get to sleep.
Went on mission to Anselles-Sur-Mer,
on French Coast. Bombed gun emplacements,
troops, etc. Carried 38 - 100 lb. demolition
bombs. 1700 gals. fuel. Bombed from 16,000'.
Invasion began at 07:25. Zero hour
was 07:30. Our group put up 42 ships in
first wave, and 12 in second. 1,350 heavy
bombers were in the first wave, &
550 in second. 11,000 planes will be over coast
during day. Some Blitz. We bombed PFF -
"Gee Bof". Mission lasted 4½ hours. We are alerted
again. Up at 15:00. Went to Thury-Harcourt,
Coast of France. Bombed in front of our landing
troops. Bombed an important road junction. Dropped
12-500 lbs. bombs. Just Group Leader (PFF) and us went
in alone. Rest of formation didn't find us. Lots of clouds.
Good ringside seat up there. Ships and boats of all kinds.
Men on beach. Fires & shell all over coast. Bombed from
17,000'. Mission 4½ hours. Landed 22:45. Plenty tired.

RCS Diary entry for July 6, 1944, original text.

Photo of the nose of the B-17 "Rose of York". From the collection of Robert J. Curran, Lead Navigator in the 306th B.G., 368th B.S., attained the rank of Captain. He was born on May 28, 1916 in Littleton, New Hampshire and died on November 13, 1997; he is buried in Waterford, Vermont. *Courtesy of the Mighty Eighth Air Force Museum.*

Royal Family at the "Rose of York" dedication. From the collection of Robert G. Shultz. *Courtesy of the Mighty Eighth Air Force Museum.*

Royal Family at the "Rose of York" dedication. From the collection of Robert G. Shultz. *Courtesy of the Mighty Eighth Air Force Museum.*

Photo of HRH Princess Elizabeth holding a bouquet of flowers, surrounded by people. Behind her is an AAF officer. On the left side is the nose of the B-17 "Rose of York." From the collection of Robert J. Curran (see caption to Figure 3-29). *Courtesy of the Mighty Eighth Air Force Museum.*

Royal Family at the "Rose of York" dedication. From the collection of Robert G. Shultz. *Courtesy of the Mighty Eighth Air Force Museum.*

"Glenn Miller" (written on scrapbook page). "Played in Hangar 4 on July 14, 1944" (written *verso* in black ink). From the collection of Robert G. Shultz. *Courtesy of the Mighty Eighth Air Force Museum.* Note that this date coincides with the July 14th entry in the RCS diary.

"Cal Kesling on the 1st Saturday inspection Some more chicken s___" (written *verso* in pencil). From the collection of Robert G. Shultz. *Courtesy of the Mighty Eighth Air Force Museum.*

Adolph Gysbert "Sailor" Malan.

IV

Robert C. Sage
The Later Years (1945-2002)

My father must have returned to Philadelphia with mixed emotions. Photographs of a handsome young officer with some of his medals (page 97), and reunited with his wife (page 98), show a mature man with a steady gaze, and perhaps a hint of sadness or resolve in his open features. His mother wrote on the back of a 1945 photo of her son: "My heart ached when I saw how he looked. They sure used him hard. He did his share" (page 99).

Lt. Sage's military medals and insignia, kindly provided by the Mighty Eighth Air Force Museum, are shown in Appendix F. His medals include the Distinguished Flying Cross, for support of operations by "heroism or extraordinary achievement while participating in an aerial flight" (http.//en.wikipedia.org/wiki/Distinguished_Flying_Cross_United_States), Air Medal with three Oak Leaf Clusters (see diary entry for August 17), American Campaign Medal, World War II Victory Medal, European-African-Middle Eastern Campaign Medal, and the Presidential Unit Citation. It seems indeed that "he did his share."

These medals and citations, however, did not bring my father the kind of life to which he had aspired. Responding to the loss of time while in the service, and to the desire for a family, at the age of 24 RCS did not re-enter college, a decision that precluded his attending medical school, but entered into the family business, Mutual Rendering Company of Philadelphia, of which his father was President. In 1946 and in 1950, respectively, a daughter, Emily Helene, and a son, Robert Charles Jr., were born, and my father moved his small family to Abington, a suburb of Philadelphia. The photographs on pages 100 and 101 show him with his young daughter in the back yard of the house (he was an avid horticulturist, specializing in roses and fruit trees) and sitting proudly in his AAF jacket on top of his stash of winter firewood. Everything he built was sturdy, beautiful, and essentially perfect, and it was clear that he was chafing under the controlled environment of the city and suburban life.

Harry Sage, a veteran of World War I, enrolled his two sons, RCS and Harry Russell, as Hereditary Life Members in the Military Order of the World Wars, a membership in perpetuity (page 102, top). This organization meant a great deal to him, especially in his final years, as he relived his war experiences and visited with surviving members of the 306th.

Photographs of my father c1958 show an executive approaching middle age (pages 102, bottom, and 103). Not revealed are the difficulties and stressful times he was experiencing at his father's company. Driven by a strong desire to be independent and to live away from the city, RCS in the next several years purchased a horse farm for his family in Berks County, Pennsylvania, and started his own rendering company, Robert C. Sage, Inc., located in nearby Boyertown. He was proud of both Spring Hill Farm, where he continued riding and learned to drive his horse Spring Hill Dolly (page 104), and his business, with its state-of-the-art equipment (page 105, top). My brother and I grew up on this farm, a beautiful place with its attendant share of hard work. It was sold less than 20 years later upon my parents' divorce and the bankruptcy of the Boyertown business.

The concept of retirement was somewhat foreign to my father, but several visits to dude ranches in Montana with his wife Dianne convinced him that settling in the West was to be a final dream fulfilled. They purchased a ranch near Livingston, Montana, and raised horses, chickens, and other assorted livestock. Horses had been an important part of my father's life, a pursuit shared with Dianne in the mountains surrounding their ranch (pages 105, bottom, through 107). The "Sage Ranch" (page 108, "So let it be") was later sold, however, and the couple moved westward to settle in Whitehall, Montana, where my father died from complications of cancer on February 20, 2002.

A few months prior to his death, my brother and I visited him in Whitehall. He spoke frequently of the war and gave us many photographs from his life (heretofore rather private), some of which have been reproduced in this book. From a life rife with disappointments, he always managed to secure for himself moments and situations of happiness. His approach to life was positive and rational, he was conservative in his political and social views (he was a strong supporter of Richard Nixon), he was creative and artistic, and his interest in animals and the land was immutable. His diary, describing a relatively small window of World War II and his sincere contribution to that effort, perhaps represented in later years his unspoken desire for a small wedge of immortality.

First Lieutenant RCS, November 23, 1945, after his discharge from the Army Air Corps in October, 1945. Note oak leaf cluster and bar.

RCS and his wife, Helen, reunited after the war.

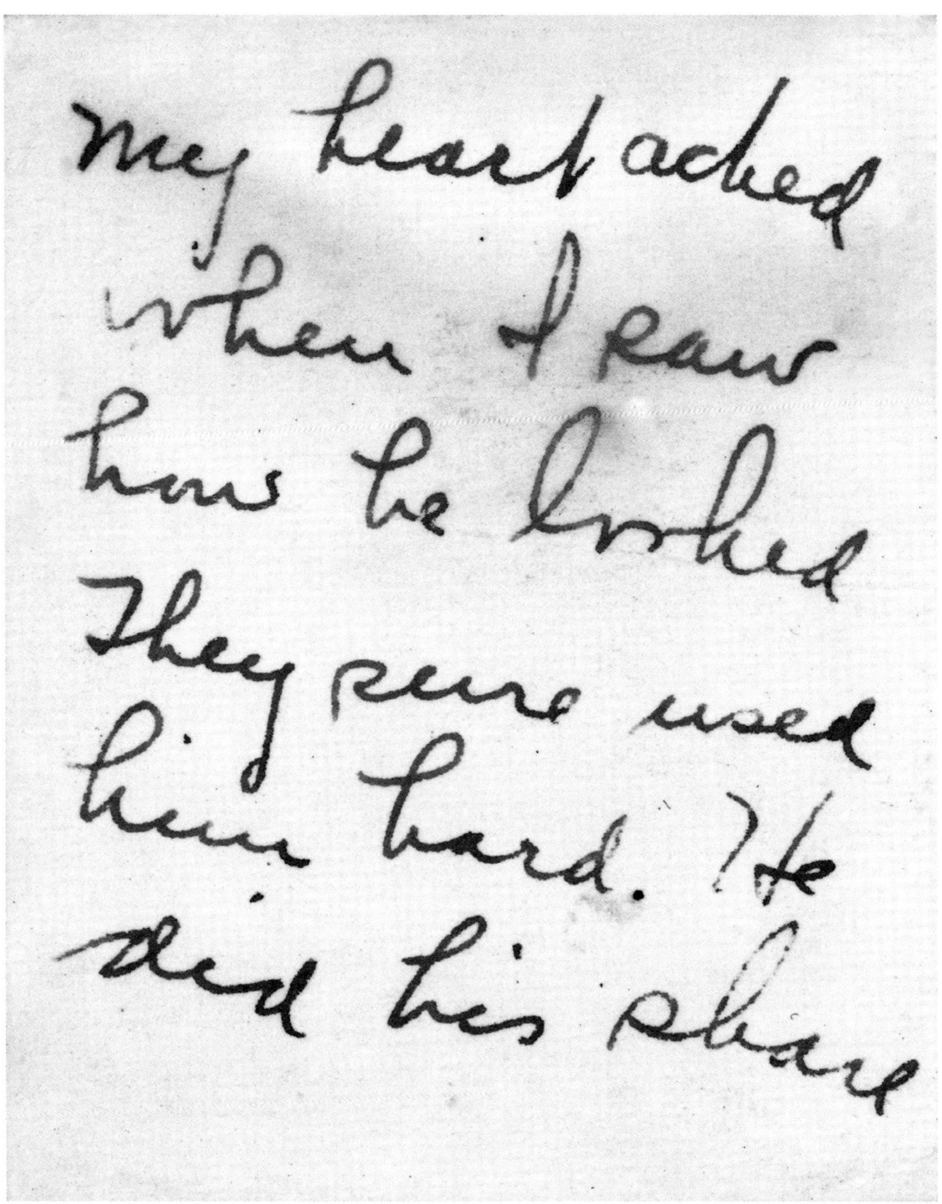

My heart ached
when I saw
how he looked
They sure used
him hard. He
did his share

Verso of photograph of RCS taken after his discharge, written by his mother: "My heart ached when I saw how he looked. They sure used him hard. He did his share."

RCS and his young daughter, Emily Helene (the author), in the backyard of their home in Abington, Pennsylvania.

RCS, retaining some military attire (see page 26 for jacket), sitting on his load of freshly-stacked wood. Abington, Pennsylvania.

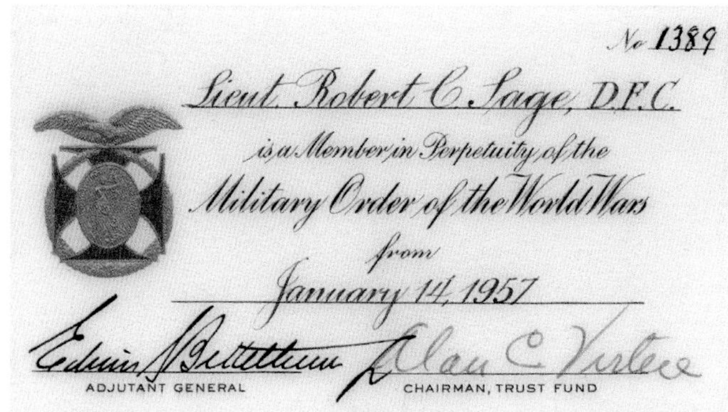

No 1389

Lieut. Robert C. Sage, D.F.C.

is a Member in Perpetuity of the

Military Order of the World Wars

from

January 14, 1957

ADJUTANT GENERAL CHAIRMAN, TRUST FUND

Membership card #1389 for the Military Order of the World Wars, an organization that meant a great deal to RCS in later years.

RCS as a young executive at Mutual Rendering Company, Philadelphia, September, 1958. A lithograph of one of his great passions, railroads and trains, is shown in the background.

RCS, a member of Rotary, International, and Vice President of Mutual Rendering Company, c1960.

Spring Hill Farm, Macungie, Pennsylvania, July, 1966. RCS in hunt attire poses with his half-Thoroughbred hunter Robin Hood. The 19th century farmhouse is shown in the background, and is there today.

RCS in the Doctor's buggy, drawn by Spring Hill Dolly, an Amish mare.

A proud moment as the new rendering business, Robert C. Sage, Inc., starts in Boyertown, Pennsylvania. This fleet of trucks was kept immaculate (rather like his aircraft of WW II!).

Halter-breaking a colt on the Sage Ranch, Livingston, Montana, 1989. *Verso:* "HALTER-BROKE (SAGE). HE IS SPOILING HER, SHE FOLLOWS HIM ALL OVER!" (written by Dianne Sage). *Photo courtesy of Dianne S. James.*

RCS on "Quill," riding Western-style, in Big Timber Canon, Montana. *Photo courtesy of Dianne S. James.*

RCS and "Quill—Slough Creek, Yellowstone Park, August 1989." *Photo courtesy of Dianne S. James.*

Entrance to "SAGE RANCH," Livingston, Montana, in winter. Note the American flag. A curious inscription in RCS's handwriting, *verso*: "So let it be—."

Appendix A:
Pilot Flight Record and Log Book

PILOT FLIGHT RECORD
AND LOG BOOK
TYPE SD-3

Aero Service & Supply Company
Municipal Airport
BIRMINGHAM, ALABAMA

IDENTIFICATION
AND LICENSE RECORD

Name SAGE, Robert C.
Address 4830 Castor Ave. Phila., Pa.
Signature Robert C. Sage
Birth Date June 14, 1921
Height 6'0"
Color Hair Blond
Color Eyes Blue
Weight 145#
Remarks

PASTE COPY OF LICENSE PHOTO HERE

CERTIFICATE OR RATINGS ISSUED	DATE ISSUED	NUMBER

DATE 19 43	FLIGHT FROM	FLIGHT TO	AIRCRAFT MAKE AND MODEL	AIRCRAFT CERTIFICATE MARK	CLASSIFICATION Horse Power	Gross Wgt.	Make Engine	DURATION OF FLIGHT Hours	Min.	LANDINGS
June 1	Decatur, Ala.	Local	Stearman PT-17	Army-200	220	2635	Continental Radial	0	33	1
2	"	"	"	" 62	"	"	"	0	52	2
3	"	"	"	" "	"	"	"	0	46	2
4	"	"	"	" "	"	"	"	0	48	1
5	"	"	"	" "	"	"	"	0	45	2
7	"	"	"	" "	"	"	"	0	54	3
8	"	"	"	" "	"	"	"	1	01	4
10	"	"	"	" 66	"	"	"	0	42	3
11	"	"	"	" 62	"	"	"	0	35	1
12	"	"	"	" "	"	"	"	0	53	5
14	"	"	"	" "	"	"	"	1	11	4
THE RECORD ON THIS PAGE IS CERTIFIED TRUE AND CORRECT:					"	"	"	09	00	28

PILOT [signature] ATTESTED BY ________

CARRY TOTALS FORWARD TO TOP OF NEXT PAGE

BREAKDOWN OF TRIP TIME INTO CLASSIFICATIONS INSTRUMENT	INSTRUCTION	DAY Hrs.	Min	NIGHT	DUAL Hrs.	Min	SOLO	REMARKS INSTRUCTOR SHOULD ENTER IN THIS COLUMN THE NATURE OF EACH MANEUVER IN WHICH INSTRUCTION IS GIVEN, AND THE TIME SPENT THEREON, AND SHALL ATTEST EACH SUCH ENTRY WITH HIS INITIALS, PILOT CERTIFICATE NUMBER, AND PERTINENT RATING.
		0	33		0	33		Orientation.
		0	52		0	52		Medium + climbing turns, S. + L. flight.
		0	46		0	46		Stalls, spins, S turns, medium + climb. turns.
		0	48		0	48		180° turns, S turns, co-ord. exercises, gliding turns
		0	45		0	45		Landings, takeoffs, turns, spins, S+L flight
		0	54		0	54		Landings, takeoffs, pattern, all turns, + glides
		1	01		1	01		Rectangular pattern, takeoffs + landings.
		0	42		0	42		Landings, takeoffs, and pattern.
		0	35		0	35		Stalls, spins, steep + med. turns, coord ex.
		0	53		0	53		Landings, takeoffs, turns. (Flat tail wheel)
		1	11		1	11		Review of everything to date in sequence
		09	00		09	00		ENTER IN THIS COLUMN DETAILS OF ANY SERIOUS DAMAGE TO AIRCRAFT. IF MORE SPACE THAN THAT PROVIDED ABOVE IS NEEDED FOR ANY DETAILS OF FLIGHT INSTRUCTION OR AIRCRAFT DAMAGE, USE PAGES PROVIDED IN BACK OF BOOK.

This time is correct and certified by me. [illegible] C.G.I. #200183

CARRY TOTALS FORWARD TO TOP OF NEXT PAGE

DATE 19 43	FLIGHT FROM	FLIGHT TO	AIRCRAFT MAKE AND MODEL	AIRCRAFT CERTIFICATE MARK	CLASSIFICATION: Horse Power	Gross Wgt.	Make Engine	DURATION OF FLIGHT: Hours (09)	Min (00)	LANDINGS
15	Decatur, Ala	Local	Stearman PT 17	Army 62	220	2635	Continental Radial	1	04	6
16	"	"	"	" "	"	"	"	1	13	7
17	"	"	"	" "	"	"	"	0	34	3
17	"	"	"	" "	"	"	"	0	24	1
17	"	"	"	" "	"	"	"	0	08	1
18	"	"	"	" "	"	"	"	0	16	2
18	"	"	"	" "	"	"	"	0	36	4
18	"	"	"	" "	"	"	"	0	15	1
19	"	"	"	" "	"	"	"	0	06	1
19	"	"	"	" "	"	"	"	0	58	3
21	"	"	"	" 203	"	"	"	0	45	3
THE RECORD ON THIS PAGE IS CERTIFIED TRUE AND CORRECT:					"	"	"	15	19	32
PILOT Robert C. Sage ATTESTED BY					CARRY TOTALS FORWARD TO TOP OF NEXT PAGE					28 / 60

BREAKDOWN OF TRIP TIME INTO CLASSIFICATIONS: INSTRUMENT		INSTRUCTION		DAY Hrs. (09)	Min (00)	NIGHT		DUAL Hrs. (09)	Min (00)	SOLO Hrs.	Min	REMARKS — INSTRUCTOR SHOULD ENTER IN THIS COLUMN THE NATURE OF EACH MANEUVER IN WHICH INSTRUCTION IS GIVEN, AND THE TIME SPENT THEREON, AND SHALL ATTEST EACH SUCH ENTRY WITH HIS INITIALS, PILOT CERTIFICATE NUMBER, AND PERTINENT RATING.
				1	04			1	04			Landings, takeoffs, and patterns
				1	13			1	13			Landings, takeoffs, & forced landings
				0	34			0	34			Landings & takeoffs.
				0	24					0	24	First solo! Storm came up.
				0	08			0	08			Returned to home field
				0	16			0	16			Landings & takeoffs.
				0	36					0	36	Landings, takeoffs, & patterns.
				0	15			0	15			Landing, takeoff, & pattern.
				0	06			0	06			Pattern.
				0	58					0	58	Pattern, landings with drift
				0	45			0	45			Mr. Lundy – P.L. [illegible]
				15	19			13	21	1	58	ENTER IN THIS COLUMN DETAILS OF ANY SERIOUS DAMAGE TO AIRCRAFT. IF MORE SPACE THAN THAT PROVIDED ABOVE IS NEEDED FOR ANY DETAILS OF FLIGHT INSTRUCTION OR AIRCRAFT DAMAGE, USE PAGES PROVIDED IN BACK OF BOOK.
CARRY TOTALS FORWARD TO TOP OF NEXT PAGE												

Air time is correct and certified by me: J. H. [illegible] C.S.I. # 20183

DATE 1943	FLIGHT FROM	FLIGHT TO	AIRCRAFT MAKE AND MODEL	AIRCRAFT CERTIFICATE MARK	CLASSIFICATION H.P.	Wgt.	MAKE Engine	DURATION OF FLIGHT		LAND.
								15	19	60
22	Decatur, Ala	Local	Stearman PT 17	Army-62	220	2635	Continental Radial	0	58	5
23	"	"	"	" "	"	"	"	1	14	10
24	"	"	"	" "	"	"	"	1	04	4
25	"	"	"	" 203	"	"	"	0	50	2
26	"	"	"	" 110	"	"	"	0	38	1
28	"	"	"	" "	"	"	"	0	53	5
30	"	"	"	" "	"	"	"	0	44	6
July 1	"	"	"	" 666	"	"	"	0	51	5
1	"	"	"	" "	"	"	"	0	41	5
1	"	"	"	" "	"	"	"	0	10	1
5	"	"	"	" 75	"	"	"	0	34	6
								23	56	110

THE RECORD ON THIS PAGE IS CERTIFIED TRUE AND CORRECT:

PILOT Robert C. Sage ATTESTED BY________

CARRY TOTALS FORWARD TO TOP OF NEXT PAGE

BREAKDOWN OF TRIP TIME INTO CLASSIFICATIONS

INSTRUMENT	INSTRUCTION	DAY		NIGHT		DUAL		SOLO		REMARKS
		15	19			13	21	1	58	INSTRUCTOR SHOULD ENTER IN THIS COLUMN THE NATURE OF EACH MANEUVER IN WHICH INSTRUCTION IS GIVEN, AND THE TIME SPENT THEREON, AND SHALL ATTEST EACH SUCH ENTRY WITH HIS INITIALS, PILOT CERTIFICATE NUMBER, AND PERTINENT RATING.
This time is correct and certified by me. [illegible] 20183		0	58			0	58			Landings, forced landings, & Rect. Course
		1	14			1	14			Landings
		1	04			1	04			Sequence
		0	50			0	50			Mr. Lundy - fl. comm. Stalls, turns, & spin, 1 forced land.
		0	38			0	38			Mr. Page - stalls, spin, & S turns.
		0	53			0	53			Mr. Page - Landings & patterns.
		0	44			0	44			Mr. Page - Landings.
		0	51			0	51			S turns, stalls, spin - Mr. R. C. Griffin
		0	41					0	41	Solo! Supervised Mr. Griffin - landings.
		0	10			0	10			Mr. Griffin -
		0	34			0	34			Landings & takeoffs Mr. John E. Anderson
		23	56			21	17	02	39	ENTER IN THIS COLUMN DETAILS OF ANY SERIOUS DAMAGE TO AIRCRAFT. IF MORE SPACE THAN THAT PROVIDED ABOVE IS NEEDED FOR ANY DETAILS OF FLIGHT INSTRUCTION OR AIRCRAFT DAMAGE, USE PAGES PROVIDED IN BACK OF BOOK.

CARRY TOTALS FORWARD TO TOP OF NEXT PAGE

BREAKDOWN OF TRIP TIME INTO CLASSIFICATIONS										REMARKS
INSTRUMENT		INSTRUCTION		DAY		NIGHT		DUAL		SOLO		INSTRUCTOR SHOULD ENTER IN THIS COLUMN THE NATURE OF EACH MANEUVER IN WHICH INSTRUCTION IS GIVEN, AND THE TIME SPENT THEREON, AND SHALL ATTEST EACH SUCH ENTRY WITH HIS INITIALS, PILOT CERTIFICATE NUMBER, AND PERTINENT RATING.
				23	56			21	17	02	39	
				0	50					0	50	Solo stage landings Home field.
				01	05			01	05			Sequence including chandelles
				01	10					01	10	Took ship off line first time. Sequence
				01	06					01	06	Sequence.
				01	15					01	15	Sequence.
				01	04			01	04			Sequence - Mr Anderson.
				01	07					01	07	Sequense.
				0	55			0	55			20 hr. check - Mr. Lundy
				0	51			0	51			Instructor - Chand. - Lazy & Pylon Eights
				01	06					01	06	
				01	02					01	02	
				35	27			25	12	10	15	ENTER IN THIS COLUMN DETAILS OF ANY SERIOUS DAMAGE TO AIRCRAFT. IF MORE SPACE THAN THAT PROVIDED ABOVE IS NEEDED FOR ANY DETAILS OF FLIGHT INSTRUCTION OR AIRCRAFT DAMAGE, USE PAGES PROVIDED IN BACK OF BOOK.
CARRY TOTALS FORWARD TO TOP OF NEXT PAGE												

DATE 1943	FLIGHT FROM	FLIGHT TO	AIRCRAFT MAKE AND MODEL	AIRCRAFT CERTIFICATE MARK	CLASSIFICATION H.P.	Wgt.	MAKE ENGINE	DURATION OF FLIGHT		LAND.
								35	27	127
July-8	Decatur Ala	Local	Stearman PT 17	Army-70	220	2635	Continental Radial	0	55	1
9	"	"	"	" 63	"	"	"	01	04	1
10	"	"	"	" "	"	"	"	0	55	3
10	"	"	"	" 84	"	"	"	01	16	1
12	"	"	"	" 90	"	"	"	01	06	1
12	"	"	"	" 103	"	"	"	01	05	1
13	"	"	"	" 202	"	"	"	01	06	1
13	"	"	"	" 108	"	"	"	01	10	1
14	"	"	"	" 203	"	"	"	01	03	1
14	"	"	"	" 202	"	"	"	01	02	1
15	"	"	"	" 63	"	"	"	0	51	1
THE RECORD ON THIS PAGE IS CERTIFIED TRUE AND CORRECT:								47	00	14
PILOT Robert C. Sage ATTESTED BY								CARRY TOTALS FORWARD TO TOP OF NEXT PAGE		

BREAKDOWN OF TRIP TIME INTO CLASSIFICATIONS										REMARKS
INSTRUMENT	INSTRUCTION	DAY		NIGHT		DUAL		SOLO		INSTRUCTOR SHOULD ENTER IN THIS COLUMN THE NATURE OF EACH MANEUVER IN WHICH INSTRUCTION IS GIVEN, AND THE TIME SPENT THEREON, AND SHALL ATTEST EACH SUCH ENTRY WITH HIS INITIALS, PILOT CERTIFICATE NUMBER, AND PERTINENT RATING.
		35	27			25	12	10	15	
		0	55					0	55	
		01	04					01	04	
		0	55			0	55			180° landings.
		01	16					01	16	
		01	06					01	06	
		01	05					01	05	
		01	06					01	06	
		01	10					01	10	
		01	03			01	03			Mr. Lundy - 40 hr. check - failed.
		01	02					01	02	
		0	51			0	51			
		47	00			28	01	18	59	ENTER IN THIS COLUMN DETAILS OF ANY SERIOUS DAMAGE TO AIRCRAFT. IF MORE SPACE THAN THAT PROVIDED ABOVE IS NEEDED FOR ANY DETAILS OF FLIGHT INSTRUCTION OR AIRCRAFT DAMAGE, USE PAGES PROVIDED IN BACK OF BOOK.
CARRY TOTALS FORWARD TO TOP OF NEXT PAGE										

DATE 1943	FLIGHT FROM	FLIGHT TO	AIRCRAFT MAKE AND MODEL	AIRCRAFT CERTIFICATE MARK	CLASSIFICATION			DURATION OF FLIGHT		LANDINGS
					H.P.	Wgt.	Make Engine	23	56	110
July 5	Decatur, Ala.	Local	Stearman PT 17	Army 75	220	2635	Continental Radial	0	50	6
5	"	"	"	" 75	"	"	"	01	05	1
5	"	"	"	" 62	"	"	"	01	10	1
6	"	"	"	" 94	"	"	"	01	06	1
6	"	"	"	" 94	"	"	"	01	15	1
6	"	"	"	" 65	"	"	"	01	04	1
7	"	"	"	" 201	"	"	"	01	07	1
7	"	"	"	" 76	"	"	"	0	55	1
8	"	"	"	" 63				0	51	1
8	"	"	"	" 63				01	06	2
8	"	"	"	" 106				01	02	1
THE RECORD ON THIS PAGE IS CERTIFIED TRUE AND CORRECT:								35	27	127
PILOT Robert C. Sage ATTESTED BY ______					CARRY TOTALS FORWARD TO TOP OF NEXT PAGE					

BREAKDOWN OF TRIP TIME INTO CLASSIFICATIONS												REMARKS
INSTRUMENT		INSTRUCTION		DAY		NIGHT		DUAL		SOLO		INSTRUCTOR SHOULD ENTER IN THIS COLUMN THE NATURE OF EACH MANEUVER IN WHICH INSTRUCTION IS GIVEN, AND THE TIME SPENT THEREON, AND SHALL ATTEST EACH SUCH ENTRY WITH HIS INITIALS, PILOT CERTIFICATE NUMBER, AND PERTINENT RATING.
				23	56			21	17	02	39	
				0	50					0	50	Solo stage landings Home field.
				01	05			01	05			Sequence including chandelles
				01	10					01	10	Took ship off line first time. Sequence.
				01	06					01	06	Sequence.
				01	15					01	15	Sequence.
				01	04			01	04			Sequence - Mr. Anderson.
				01	07					01	07	Sequense.
				0	55			0	55			20 hr. check - Mr. Lundy.
				0	51			0	51			Instructor - Chand. - Lazy & Pylon Eights
				01	06					01	06	
				01	02					01	02	
				35	27			25	12	10	15	ENTER IN THIS COLUMN DETAILS OF ANY SERIOUS DAMAGE TO AIRCRAFT. IF MORE SPACE THAN THAT PROVIDED ABOVE IS NEEDED FOR ANY DETAILS OF FLIGHT INSTRUCTION OR AIRCRAFT DAMAGE, USE PAGES PROVIDED IN BACK OF BOOK.
CARRY TOTALS FORWARD TO TOP OF NEXT PAGE												

DATE 1943	FLIGHT FROM	FLIGHT TO	AIRCRAFT MAKE AND MODEL	AIRCRAFT CERTIFICATE MARK	CLASSIFICATION H.P.	Wgt	MAKE ENGINE	DURATION OF FLIGHT		LAND.
								35	27	127
July - 8	Decatur, Ala	Local	Stearman PT 17	Army-70	220	2635	Continental Radial	0	55	1
9	..	..	..	.. 63	..	..	..	01	04	1
10	..	..	..	.. ..	..	..	..	0	55	3
10	..	..	..	.. 84	..	..	..	01	16	1
12	..	..	..	.. 90	..	..	..	01	06	1
12	..	..	..	.. 103	..	..	..	01	05	1
13	..	..	..	.. 202	..	..	..	01	06	1
13	..	..	..	.. 108	..	..	..	01	10	1
14	..	..	..	.. 203	..	..	..	01	03	1
14	..	..	..	.. 202	..	..	..	01	02	1
15	..	..	..	.. 63	..	..	..	0	51	1
THE RECORD ON THIS PAGE IS CERTIFIED TRUE AND CORRECT:								47	00	14[illegible]
PILOT Robert C. Sage ATTESTED BY					CARRY TOTALS FORWARD TO TOP OF NEXT PAGE					

BREAKDOWN OF TRIP TIME INTO CLASSIFICATIONS												REMARKS INSTRUCTOR SHOULD ENTER IN THIS COLUMN THE NATURE OF EACH MANEUVER IN WHICH INSTRUCTION IS GIVEN, AND THE TIME SPENT THEREON, AND SHALL ATTEST EACH SUCH ENTRY WITH HIS INITIALS, PILOT CERTIFICATE NUMBER, AND PERTINENT RATING.
INSTRUMENT		INSTRUCTION		DAY		NIGHT		DUAL		SOLO		
				35	27			25	12	10	15	
				0	55					0	55	
				01	04					01	04	
				0	55			0	55			180° landings.
				01	16					01	16	
				01	06					01	06	
				01	05					01	05	
				01	06					01	06	
				01	10					01	10	
				01	03			01	03			Mr. Lundy - 40 hr. check - failed.
				01	02					01	02	
				0	51			0	51			
				47	00			28	01	18	59	ENTER IN THIS COLUMN DETAILS OF ANY SERIOUS DAMAGE TO AIRCRAFT. IF MORE SPACE THAN THAT PROVIDED ABOVE IS NEEDED FOR ANY DETAILS OF FLIGHT INSTRUCTION OR AIRCRAFT DAMAGE, USE PAGES PROVIDED IN BACK OF BOOK.
CARRY TOTALS FORWARD TO TOP OF NEXT PAGE												

DATE 1943	FLIGHT FROM	FLIGHT TO	AIRCRAFT MAKE AND MODEL	AIRCRAFT CERTIFICATE MARK	CLASSIFICATION			DURATION OF FLIGHT		LAND.
					H.P.	Wgt.	MAKE ENGINE	47	00	140
July-15	Decatur Ala	Local	Stearman PT-17	Army 220	220	2635	Continental Radial	0	36	1
15	"	"	"	" 69	"	"	"	01	04	1
16	"	"	"	" 63	"	"	"	0	49	1
16	"	"	"	" "	"	"	"	01	13	1
16	"	"	"	" 82	"	"	"	01	06	1
17	"	Cullman-Arab and return.	"	" 90	"	"	"	01	08	1
17	"	Local	"	" 91	"	"	"	01	16	3
19	"	"	"	" 63	"	"	"	01	15	13
20	"	Hartselle to Guntersville Dam & return	"	" 94	"	"	"	0	55	1
20	"	Local	"	" 106	"	"	"	0	46	1
21	"	"	"	" 77	"	"	"	0	54	7
THE RECORD ON THIS PAGE IS CERTIFIED TRUE AND CORRECT:								58	02	171
PILOT Robert C. Sage		ATTESTED BY			CARRY TOTALS FORWARD TO TOP OF NEXT PAGE					

BREAKDOWN OF TRIP TIME INTO CLASSIFICATIONS

INSTRUMENT	INSTRUCTION	DAY	NIGHT	DUAL	SOLO	REMARKS
		47 00		28 01	18 59	INSTRUCTOR SHOULD ENTER IN THIS COLUMN THE NATURE OF EACH MANEUVER IN WHICH INSTRUCTION IS GIVEN, AND THE TIME SPENT THEREON, AND SHALL ATTEST EACH SUCH ENTRY WITH HIS INITIALS, PILOT CERTIFICATE NUMBER, AND PERTINENT RATING.
		0 36		0 36		Army check - Lt. Newton Reelorst - passed
		01 04			01 04	
		0 49		0 49		
		01 13			01 13	
		01 06			01 06	
		01 08			01 08	Cross-country - (dual.)
		01 16		01 16		Check ride - Mr. Page.
		01 15		01 15		Hurdle & Cross-wind stages.
		0 55			0 55	Solo cross-country.
		0 46			0 46	
		0 54			0 54	180° stage.
CARRY TOTALS FORWARD TO TOP OF NEXT PAGE		58 02		31 57	26 05	ENTER IN THIS COLUMN DETAILS OF ANY SERIOUS DAMAGE TO AIRCRAFT. IF MORE SPACE THAN THAT PROVIDED ABOVE IS NEEDED FOR ANY DETAILS OF FLIGHT INSTRUCTION OR AIRCRAFT DAMAGE, USE PAGES PROVIDED IN BACK OF BOOK.

DATE 1943	FLIGHT FROM	FLIGHT TO	AIRCRAFT MAKE AND MODEL	AIRCRAFT CERTIFICATE MARK	CLASSIFICATION: H. P.	Wgt	MAKE ENGINE	DURATION OF FLIGHT	LAND.
								58 02	171
July 21	Decatur, Ala	Local	Stearman PT 17	Army-63	220	2635	Consolidated Radial	0 50	1
22	"	"	"	" 104	"	"	"	0 46	1
22	"	"	"	" 109	"	"	"	0 42	1
23	"	"	"	" "	"	"	"	01 00	8
23	"	"	"	" 203	"	"	"	0 44	1
				165	94	- 40			
THE RECORD ON THIS PAGE IS CERTIFIED TRUE AND CORRECT:								62 04	183
PILOT Robert C. Page	ATTESTED BY				CARRY TOTALS FORWARD TO TOP OF NEXT PAGE				

John E. Henderson
Army Primary
From June 1st to July 23 1943

BREAKDOWN OF TRIP TIME INTO CLASSIFICATIONS												REMARKS INSTRUCTOR SHOULD ENTER IN THIS COLUMN THE NATURE OF EACH MANEUVER IN WHICH INSTRUCTION IS GIVEN, AND THE TIME SPENT THEREON, AND SHALL ATTEST EACH SUCH ENTRY WITH HIS INITIALS, PILOT CERTIFICATE NUMBER, AND PERTINENT RATING.
INSTRUMENT		INSTRUCTION		DAY		NIGHT		DUAL		SOLO		
				58	02			31	57	26	05	
				0	50			0	50			Acrobatics.
				0	46					0	46	
				0	42					0	42	
				01	00			01	00			Front seat ride. Wheel landings.
				0	44			0	44			60 hr. check. Passed! Mr. Lundy
				62	04			34	31	27	33	ENTER IN THIS COLUMN DETAILS OF ANY SERIOUS DAMAGE TO AIRCRAFT. IF MORE SPACE THAN THAT PROVIDED ABOVE IS NEEDED FOR ANY DETAILS OF FLIGHT INSTRUCTION OR AIRCRAFT DAMAGE, USE PAGES PROVIDED IN BACK OF BOOK.

CARRY TOTALS FORWARD TO TOP OF NEXT PAGE

DATE 1943	FLIGHT FROM	FLIGHT TO	AIRCRAFT MAKE AND MODEL	AIRCRAFT CERTIFICATE MARK	CLASSIFICATION			DURATION OF FLIGHT		LANDING
Aug. 3	Courtland, Ala	Local	Valtee-BT 13A	Army-317				01	00	1
4	"	"	" " "	" "				0	55	1
6	"	"	" "	" "				0	55	1
8	"	"	" "	" 318				0	50	1
10	"	"	" "	" "				0	40	3
11	"	"	" "	" 346				0	35	4
11	"	"	" "	" "				0	25	3
11	"	"	" "	" "				0	20	1
12	"	"	" "	" 339				01	10	1
15	"	"	" "	" 306				0	55	1
15	"	"	" "	" 336				01	—	8
								08	45	25

THE RECORD ON THIS PAGE IS CERTIFIED TRUE AND CORRECT:

PILOT Robert C. Sage ATTESTED BY__________

CARRY TOTALS FORWARD TO TOP OF NEXT PAGE

BREAKDOWN OF TRIP TIME INTO CLASSIFICATIONS						REMARKS INSTRUCTOR SHOULD ENTER IN THIS COLUMN THE NATURE OF EACH MANEUVER IN WHICH INSTRUCTION IS GIVEN, AND THE TIME SPENT THEREON, AND SHALL ATTEST EACH SUCH ENTRY WITH HIS INITIALS, PILOT CERTIFICATE NUMBER, AND PERTINENT RATING.
INSTRUMENT	INSTRUCTION	DAY	NIGHT	DUAL	SOLO	
		01 00		01 00		Orientation ride. Inst.-2nd Lt. Van H. Burrows [?]
		0 55		0 55		Cord. Q. St. & nrl. turns. Stalls. Spin [?] (cl. 2 bl. [?])
		0 55		0 55		
		0 50		0 50		
		0 40		0 40		
		0 35		0 35		
		0 25			0 25	First solo in the BT 13A.
		0 20		0 20		
		01 10			01 10	
		0 55		0 55		
		01 [blacked out]			01 [blacked out]	90° stage -
		08 45		06 10	02 35	ENTER IN THIS COLUMN DETAILS OF ANY SERIOUS DAMAGE TO AIRCRAFT. IF MORE SPACE THAN THAT PROVIDED ABOVE IS NEEDED FOR ANY DETAILS OF FLIGHT INSTRUCTION OR AIRCRAFT DAMAGE, USE PAGES PROVIDED IN BACK OF BOOK.
CARRY TOTALS FORWARD TO TOP OF NEXT PAGE						

DATE 1943	FLIGHT FROM	FLIGHT TO	AIRCRAFT MAKE AND MODEL	AIRCRAFT CERTIFICATE MARK	CLASSIFICATION			DURATION OF FLIGHT	LAND.
								08 45	25
17	Courtland, Ala.	Local	Vultee-BT13A	Army-307				01 20	1
19	"	"	" "	" 337				0 25	1
20	"	"	" "	" 306				0 50	6
21	"	"	" "	" 307				01 —	1
23	"	"	" "	" 306				0 35	1
24	"	"	" "	" 337				0 30	1
25	"	"	" "	" 319				01 10	1
25	"	"	" "	" 324				01 —	6
26	"	"	" "	" 344				01 05	1
27	"	"	" "	" 337				01 05	1
29	"	"	" "	" 321				01 —	1
								18 45	46

THE RECORD ON THIS PAGE IS CERTIFIED TRUE AND CORRECT:

PILOT *Robert C. Sage* ATTESTED BY__________

CARRY TOTALS FORWARD TO TOP OF NEXT PAGE

BREAKDOWN OF TRIP TIME INTO CLASSIFICATIONS												REMARKS INSTRUCTOR SHOULD ENTER IN THIS COLUMN THE NATURE OF EACH MANEUVER IN WHICH INSTRUCTION IS GIVEN, AND THE TIME SPENT THEREON, AND SHALL ATTEST EACH SUCH ENTRY WITH HIS INITIALS, PILOT CERTIFICATE NUMBER, AND PERTINENT RATING.
INSTRUMENT		INSTRUCTION		DAY		NIGHT		DUAL		SOLO		
				08	45			06	10	02	35	
				01	20			01	20			Chandelles, lazy eights, Forced land. Simulated
				0	25			0	25			
				0	50			0	50			Power approaches.
				01	–			01	–			
				0	35			0	35			
0	25	~~0~~	~~05~~	0	30			0	30			0:05 T Under the hood. Orientation ride.
				01	10					01	10	
				01	–					01	–	90° stages.
01	–	~~0~~	~~05~~	01	05			01	05			0:05 T
01	–	~~0~~	~~05~~	01	05			01	05			0:05 T
				01	–					01	–	01:00 T
02	25			18	45			13	[illegible]	05	45	ENTER IN THIS COLUMN DETAILS OF ANY SERIOUS DAMAGE TO AIRCRAFT. IF MORE SPACE THAN THAT PROVIDED ABOVE IS NEEDED FOR ANY DETAILS OF FLIGHT INSTRUCTION OR AIRCRAFT DAMAGE, USE PAGES PROVIDED IN BACK OF BOOK.
CARRY TOTALS FORWARD TO TOP OF NEXT PAGE												

DATE 1943	FLIGHT FROM	FLIGHT TO	AIRCRAFT MAKE AND MODEL	AIRCRAFT CERTIFICATE MARK	CLASSIFICATION			DURATION OF FLIGHT		LAND.
								18	45	46
30	Courtland, Ala.	Corinth, Ala. & return.	Vultee-BT13A	Army-343				01	35	2
30	"	Local	" "	" 332				01	35	1
31	"	"	" "	" 309				01	–	1
31	"	"	" "	" 335				01	–	1
Sept. 1	"	"	" "	" 343				01	05	1
1	"	"	" "	" 530				0	40	1
2	"	"	" "	" 301				01	–	1
5	"	"	" "	" 326				01	–	4
5	"	"	" "	" 326				01	–	4
7	"	"	" "	" 343				01	05	1
7	"	"	" "	" 346				01	40	1
THE RECORD ON THIS PAGE IS CERTIFIED TRUE AND CORRECT:								31	25	64
PILOT Robert C. Sage ATTESTED BY					CARRY TOTALS FORWARD TO TOP OF NEXT PAGE					

BREAKDOWN OF TRIP TIME INTO CLASSIFICATIONS												REMARKS
INSTRUMENT		INSTRUCTION		DAY		NIGHT		DUAL		SOLO		INSTRUCTOR SHOULD ENTER IN THIS COLUMN THE NATURE OF EACH MANEUVER IN WHICH INSTRUCTION IS GIVEN, AND THE TIME SPENT THEREON, AND SHALL ATTEST EACH SUCH ENTRY WITH HIS INITIALS, PILOT CERTIFICATE NUMBER, AND PERTINENT RATING.
02	25			18	45			13	—	05	45	
0	55			01	35			01	35			0:40 Nav. Cross-country
				01	35					01	35	T.
				01	—					01	—	T.
				01	—					01	—	T.
01	—			01	05			01	05			0:05 T.
				0	40					0	40	T.
01	—			01	—			01	—			
						01	—	01	—			Night flying. (Flood lights & wing li[illegible])
						01	—			01	—	" " " " " "
01	—			01	05			01	05			0:05 Instruments. Patterns.
				01	40					01	40	T.
06	20			29	25	02	—	18	45	12	40	ENTER IN THIS COLUMN DETAILS OF ANY SERIOUS DAMAGE TO AIRCRAFT. IF MORE SPACE THAN THAT PROVIDED ABOVE IS NEEDED FOR ANY DETAILS OF FLIGHT INSTRUCTION OR AIRCRAFT DAMAGE, USE PAGES PROVIDED IN BACK OF BOOK.

CARRY TOTALS FORWARD TO TOP OF NEXT PAGE

DATE 1943	FLIGHT FROM	FLIGHT TO	AIRCRAFT MAKE AND MODEL	AIRCRAFT CERTIFICATE MARK	CLASSIFICATION			DURATION OF FLIGHT		LAND.
								31	25	64
8	Courtland, Ala.	Jack's Creek to Corinth & return.	Vultee-BT-13A	Army-346				02	[illegible]	1
8	"	Local	" "	" 314				0	45	1
8	"	"	" "	" 509				02	—	8
9	"	Jack's Creek to Corinth & return.	" "	" 322				[illegible]	10	1
9	"	Local	" "	" 322				01	30	1
10	"	"	" "	" 337				01	05	3
10	"	"	" "	" 311				02	—	8
11	"	"	" "	" 312				01	05	1
11	"	"	" "	" 343				01	10	1
12	"	Aberdeen, to Jasper & return.	" "	" 310				02	—	1
12	"	Local	" "	" 343				01	05	1
								46	15	91

THE RECORD ON THIS PAGE IS CERTIFIED TRUE AND CORRECT:

PILOT Robert C. Sage ATTESTED BY______

CARRY TOTALS FORWARD TO TOP OF NEXT PAGE

BREAKDOWN OF TRIP TIME INTO CLASSIFICATIONS												REMARKS
INSTRUMENT		INSTRUCTION		DAY		NIGHT		DUAL		SOLO		INSTRUCTOR SHOULD ENTER IN THIS COLUMN THE NATURE OF EACH MANEUVER IN WHICH INSTRUCTION IS GIVEN, AND THE TIME SPENT THEREON, AND SHALL ATTEST EACH SUCH ENTRY WITH HIS INITIALS, PILOT CERTIFICATE NUMBER, AND PERTINENT RATING.
06	20			29	25	02	–	18	45	12	40	
02	–			02				0		02	–	. X-Country.
0	40			0	45			0	45			0:05 DUAL T.
						02	–			02	–	Night flying. (Wing lights.)
					10				–	0	10	T.
				01	30					01	30	T.
				01	05					01	05	Nav. Short field landings.
						02	–			02	–	Night flying. (No lights.)
				01	05					01	05	T.
01	05			01	10			01	10			0:05 T.
02	–			02	–					02	–	X-Country.
01	–			01	05			01	05			0:05 T.
13	05			40	15	06	–	21	45	24	30	ENTER IN THIS COLUMN DETAILS OF ANY SERIOUS DAMAGE TO AIRCRAFT. IF MORE SPACE THAN THAT PROVIDED ABOVE IS NEEDED FOR ANY DETAILS OF FLIGHT INSTRUCTION OR AIRCRAFT DAMAGE, USE PAGES PROVIDED IN BACK OF BOOK.
CARRY TOTALS FORWARD TO TOP OF NEXT PAGE												

DATE 1943	FLIGHT FROM	FLIGHT TO	AIRCRAFT MAKE AND MODEL	AIRCRAFT CERTIFICATE MARK	CLASSIFICATION			DURATION OF FLIGHT		LAND.
								46	15	91
12	Courtland, Ala.	Local	Vultee-BT13A	Army-321				0	50	1
13	"	Oxford & return.	"	" 514				02	30	2
14	"	Local	"	" 338				02	05	2
17	"	"	"	" 337				01	30	1
22	"	"	"	" 314				0	30	1
22	"	"	"	" 313				01	50	1
23	"	"	"	" 334				01	20	1
23	"	"	"	" 317				02	05	1
24	"	"	"	" 339				01	05	1
24	"	Graham to Corinth & return.	"	" 608				02	30	1
26	"	Crossville to Smithville	"	" 337				01	30	1
THE RECORD ON THIS PAGE IS CERTIFIED TRUE AND CORRECT:								64	–	104
PILOT Robert C. Sage ATTESTED BY					CARRY TOTALS FORWARD TO TOP OF NEXT PAGE					

BREAKDOWN OF TRIP TIME INTO CLASSIFICATIONS												REMARKS
INSTRUMENT		INSTRUCTION		DAY		NIGHT		DUAL		SOLO		INSTRUCTOR SHOULD ENTER IN THIS COLUMN THE NATURE OF EACH MANEUVER IN WHICH INSTRUCTION IS GIVEN, AND THE TIME SPENT THEREON, AND SHALL ATTEST EACH SUCH ENTRY WITH HIS INITIALS, PILOT CERTIFICATE NUMBER, AND PERTINENT RATING.
13	05			40	15	06	—	21	45	24	30	
				0	50					0	50	T.
				02	30					02	30	Nav.
				02	05			02	05			02:05 – Formation flying.
				01	30					01	30	T.
				0	30			0	30			T. 40 hr. check – Lt. R.C. Moore.
				01	50					01	50	T.
				01	20					01	20	T.
				02	05					02	05	Formation.
				01	05			01	05			Acrobatics. Lt. Shockley.
						02	30			02	30	X-Country.
				01	30			01	30			X-Country – Lt. Nicoloff
13	05			55	30	08	30	26	55	37	05	ENTER IN THIS COLUMN DETAILS OF ANY SERIOUS DAMAGE TO AIRCRAFT. IF MORE SPACE THAN THAT PROVIDED ABOVE IS NEEDED FOR ANY DETAILS OF FLIGHT INSTRUCTION OR AIRCRAFT DAMAGE, USE PAGES PROVIDED IN BACK OF BOOK.
CARRY TOTALS FORWARD TO TOP OF NEXT PAGE												

DATE 1943	FLIGHT FROM	FLIGHT TO	AIRCRAFT MAKE AND MODEL	AIRCRAFT CERTIFICATE MARK	CLASSIFICATION			DURATION OF FLIGHT		LAND.
								64	—	104
26	Smithville, Tenn.	Courtland, Ala.	Vultee-BT13A	Army-331				01	10	1
27	Courtland, Ala.	Local	" "	" "				0	30	1
27	"	"	" "	" 300				01	30	2
28	"	"	" "	" 326				01	—	1
28	"	"	" "	" 302				01	—	1
28	"	"	" "	" 326				01	—	1
28	"	"	" "	" 541				01	30	1
THE RECORD ON THIS PAGE IS CERTIFIED TRUE AND CORRECT: PILOT Robert G. Sage ATTESTED BY								71	40	112
					CARRY TOTALS FORWARD TO TOP OF NEXT PAGE					

BREAKDOWN OF TRIP TIME INTO CLASSIFICATIONS												REMARKS INSTRUCTOR SHOULD ENTER IN THIS COLUMN THE NATURE OF EACH MANEUVER IN WHICH INSTRUCTION IS GIVEN, AND THE TIME SPENT THEREON, AND SHALL ATTEST EACH SUCH ENTRY WITH HIS INITIALS, PILOT CERTIFICATE NUMBER, AND PERTINENT RATING.
INSTRUMENT		INSTRUCTION		DAY		NIGHT		DUAL		SOLO		
13	05			55	30	08	30	26	55	37	05	
				01	10			01	10			X-Country – Lt. Nicoloff.
				0	30			0	30			T. Lt. R.C. Moore – 40 hr. check.
				01	30			01	30			T. Lt. G. C. Nicoloff.
				01	–			01	–			Acrobatics – dual – Lt. J. C. Murray.
0	55			01	–			01	–			0:05 T. Instr. check – Lt. Jones.
				01	–					01	–	Acrobatics.
				01	30					01	30	Acrobatics.
14	–			63	10	08	30	32	05	39	35	ENTER IN THIS COLUMN DETAILS OF ANY SERIOUS DAMAGE TO AIRCRAFT. IF MORE SPACE THAN THAT PROVIDED ABOVE IS NEEDED FOR ANY DETAILS OF FLIGHT INSTRUCTION OR AIRCRAFT DAMAGE, USE PAGES PROVIDED IN BACK OF BOOK.
CARRY TOTALS FORWARD TO TOP OF NEXT PAGE												

Aug 3, 1943 to Sept 30 Harry S. Barnes 2nd Lt. A.C. O-802974

DATE 1943	FLIGHT FROM	FLIGHT TO	AIRCRAFT MAKE AND MODEL	AIRCRAFT CERTIFICATE MARK	CLASSIFICATION			DURATION OF FLIGHT		LANDINGS
Oct. 7	Seymour, Ind.	Local	Beechcraft-AT10	Army-251				01	–	1
8	"	"	"	" 401				02	15	5
11	"	"	"	" 444				01	55	9
15	"	"	"	" 408				01	30	4
17	"	"	"	" 426				02	–	4
18	"	"	"	" 433				01	–	3
19	"	"	"	" 446						
20	"	"	"	" 423				01	40	1
21	"	"	"	" 445				01	15	2
22	"	"	"	" 409				01	15	3
23	"	"	"	" 423				01	40	1
THE RECORD ON THIS PAGE IS CERTIFIED TRUE AND CORRECT:								15	30	33
PILOT Robert C. Sage		ATTESTED BY			CARRY TOTALS FORWARD TO TOP OF NEXT PAGE					

BREAKDOWN OF TRIP TIME INTO CLASSIFICATIONS: INSTRUMENT		~~INSTRUCTION~~ CO-PILOT		DAY		NIGHT		DUAL		SOLO		REMARKS — INSTRUCTOR SHOULD ENTER IN THIS COLUMN THE NATURE OF EACH MANEUVER IN WHICH INSTRUCTION IS GIVEN, AND THE TIME SPENT THEREON, AND SHALL ATTEST EACH SUCH ENTRY WITH HIS INITIALS, PILOT CERTIFICATE NUMBER, AND PERTINENT RATING.
0	50			01	—			01	—			0:10 T. Instr. check Capt. Dave T. Smith
				02	15			02	15			T. Lt. Brooks
				01	55			01	55			T. Lt. Brooks.
				01	30			01	30			T. [illegible]
		02	—	02	—					02	—	T. Stalls, single engine procedure & landings
		02	30	01	—					01	—	T. [illegible]
		02	30									T.
01	30			01	40			01	40			0:10 T.
		01	15	01	15					01	15	T.
		01	15	01	15					01	15	T.
01	30			01	40			01	40			0:10 T.
03	50	09	30	15	30			10	—	05	30	ENTER IN THIS COLUMN DETAILS OF ANY SERIOUS DAMAGE TO AIRCRAFT. IF MORE SPACE THAN THAT PROVIDED ABOVE IS NEEDED FOR ANY DETAILS OF FLIGHT INSTRUCTION OR AIRCRAFT DAMAGE, USE PAGES PROVIDED IN BACK OF BOOK.

CARRY TOTALS FORWARD TO TOP OF NEXT PAGE

DATE 1943	FLIGHT FROM	FLIGHT TO	AIRCRAFT MAKE AND MODEL	AIRCRAFT CERTIFICATE MARK	CLASSIFICATION			DURATION OF FLIGHT		LAND.
								15	30	33
24	Seymour, Ind.	Local	Beechcraft AT10	Army-226				01	30	4
25	"	"	"	" 323				01	—	5
27	"	"	"	" 414				0	55	1
27	"	"	"	" "				0	45	—
28	"	"	"	" 436				01	10	1
28	"	"	"	" "				01	—	5
29	"	Rushville, Terre Haute, & return	"	" 432						
29	"	Local	"	" "						
30	"	"	"	" "				02	—	1
31	"	Richmond, Lexington & return	"	" 412				02	15	1
31	"	Local	"	" 410						
								26	05	51

THE RECORD ON THIS PAGE IS CERTIFIED TRUE AND CORRECT:

PILOT Robert C. Sage ATTESTED BY ____________

CARRY TOTALS FORWARD TO TOP OF NEXT PAGE

BREAKDOWN OF TRIP TIME INTO CLASSIFICATIONS												REMARKS
INSTRUMENT		~~INSTRUCTION~~ CO-PILOT		DAY		NIGHT		DUAL		SOLO		INSTRUCTOR SHOULD ENTER IN THIS COLUMN THE NATURE OF EACH MANEUVER IN WHICH INSTRUCTION IS GIVEN, AND THE TIME SPENT THEREON, AND SHALL ATTEST EACH SUCH ENTRY WITH HIS INITIALS, PILOT CERTIFICATE NUMBER, AND PERTINENT RATING.
03	50	09	30	15	30			10	—	05	30	
				01	30					01	30	T.
0	50	01	—	01	—			01	—			0:10 T.
0	45	0	45	0	55					0	55	0:10 T
0	45	0	55	0	45					0	45	
01	—	01	—	01	10					01	10	0:10 T.
				01	—					01	—	T.
		02	—									X-C.
		01	—									Instr.
				02	—			02	—			Formation.
				02	15			02	15			X-C - "NAVIGATION."
		0	45									T.
07	10	16	55	26	05			15	15	10	50	ENTER IN THIS COLUMN DETAILS OF ANY SERIOUS DAMAGE TO AIRCRAFT. IF MORE SPACE THAN THAT PROVIDED ABOVE IS NEEDED FOR ANY DETAILS OF FLIGHT INSTRUCTION OR AIRCRAFT DAMAGE, USE PAGES PROVIDED IN BACK OF BOOK.
CARRY TOTALS FORWARD TO TOP OF NEXT PAGE												

DATE 1943	FLIGHT FROM	FLIGHT TO	AIRCRAFT MAKE AND MODEL	AIRCRAFT CERTIFICATE MARK	CLASSIFICATION	DURATION OF FLIGHT		LAND
						26	05	51
Nov. 1	Seymour, Ind.	Local	Beechcraft AT10	Army-446		01	10	1
1	"	"	"	" 446		01	20	5
2	"	PRINCETON TO TERRE HAUTE & return.	"	" 404		02	10	1
2	"	Local	"	" "				
3	"	"	"	" 449		01	30	1
3	"	"	"	" "				
3	"	"	"	" 443		01	10	1
4	"	"	"	" 449		0	30	
5	"	"	"	" 343		01	10	1
8	"	Walnut Ridge	"	" 207				
8	Walnut Ridge	Monroe, La.	"	" 207		02	10	1
THE RECORD ON THIS PAGE IS CERTIFIED TRUE AND CORRECT:						37	15	62
PILOT Robert C. Sage	ATTESTED BY				CARRY TOTALS FORWARD TO TOP OF NEXT PAGE			

BREAKDOWN OF TRIP TIME INTO CLASSIFICATIONS												REMARKS
INSTRUMENT		~~INSTRUCTION~~ Co-Pilot		DAY		NIGHT		DUAL		SOLO		INSTRUCTOR SHOULD ENTER IN THIS COLUMN THE NATURE OF EACH MANEUVER IN WHICH INSTRUCTION IS GIVEN, AND THE TIME SPENT THEREON, AND SHALL ATTEST EACH SUCH ENTRY WITH HIS INITIALS, PILOT CERTIFICATE NUMBER, AND PERTINENT RATING.
07	10	16	55	26	05			15	15	10	50	
01	—	01	—	01	10					01	10	0:10 T.
				01	20					01	20	T.
02	—			02	10					02	10	0:10 T. X-C.
		0	50									Instr.
01	20			01	30					01	30	0:10 T.
		01	30									Instr.
01	—			01	10			01	10			0:10 T.
0	30	01	15	0	30					0	30	Instr.
01	—			01	10					01	10	0:10 T.
		02	50									X-C.
				02	10					02	10	X-C. Nav.
14	—	24	20	37	15			16	25	20	50	ENTER IN THIS COLUMN DETAILS OF ANY SERIOUS DAMAGE TO AIRCRAFT. IF MORE SPACE THAN THAT PROVIDED ABOVE IS NEEDED FOR ANY DETAILS OF FLIGHT INSTRUCTION OR AIRCRAFT DAMAGE, USE PAGES PROVIDED IN BACK OF BOOK.

CARRY TOTALS FORWARD TO TOP OF NEXT PAGE

DATE 1943	FLIGHT FROM	FLIGHT TO	AIRCRAFT MAKE AND MODEL	AIRCRAFT CERTIFICATE MARK	CLASSIFICATION			DURATION OF FLIGHT		LAND.
								37	15	62
Nov. 10	Selman Field, La.	Courtland, Ala.	Beechcraft AT 10	Army-207				02	45	1
10	Courtland, Ala.	FAAF	"	" "						
11	Seymour, Ind.	Local	"	" 230				01	40	1
12	"	"	"	" 406				01	30	8
12	"	Rushville, Terre Haute, & return	"	" "				02	10	1
13	"	Bloom. Ind. Rushville & return.	"	" 451				01	30	1
13	"	Muncie & return	"	" 451						
14	"	Richmond - Ind. Bloom. & return	"	" 451				02	—	1
14	"	Local	"	" 434						
16	"	"	"	" 428						
16	"	"	"	" "				02	—	6
								50	50	81

THE RECORD ON THIS PAGE IS CERTIFIED TRUE AND CORRECT:

PILOT Robert C. [illegible] ATTESTED BY ____________

CARRY TOTALS FORWARD TO TOP OF NEXT PAGE

BREAKDOWN OF TRIP TIME INTO CLASSIFICATIONS

INSTRUMENT		CO-PILOT		DAY		NIGHT		DUAL		SOLO		REMARKS
14	-	24	20	37	15			16	25	20	50	INSTRUCTOR SHOULD ENTER IN THIS COLUMN THE NATURE OF EACH MANEUVER IN WHICH INSTRUCTION IS GIVEN, AND THE TIME SPENT THEREON, AND SHALL ATTEST EACH SUCH ENTRY WITH HIS INITIALS, PILOT CERTIFICATE NUMBER, AND PERTINENT RATING.
				02	45					02	45	X-C. Nav.
		02	-									X-C. Nav.
01	30			01	40			01	40			0:10 T.
						01	30	01	30			T.
						02	10	02	10			X-C. Nav.
						01	30			01	30	X-C. Nav.
		02	-									X-C. Nav. Night.
						02	-			02	-	X-C. Nav.
		01	20									Instr.
		02	10									Night Trans.
						02	-			02	-	Night Trans.
15	30	31	50	41	40	09	10	21	45	29	05	ENTER IN THIS COLUMN DETAILS OF ANY SERIOUS DAMAGE TO AIRCRAFT. IF MORE SPACE THAN THAT PROVIDED ABOVE IS NEEDED FOR ANY DETAILS OF FLIGHT INSTRUCTION OR AIRCRAFT DAMAGE, USE PAGES PROVIDED IN BACK OF BOOK.

CARRY TOTALS FORWARD TO TOP OF NEXT PAGE

DATE 1943	FLIGHT FROM	FLIGHT TO	AIRCRAFT MAKE AND MODEL	AIRCRAFT CERTIFICATE MARK	CLASSIFICATION	DURATION OF FLIGHT	
						50	50
Nov. 17	Seymour, Ind.	Local	Beechcraft AT-10	Army 223		01	—
17	"	Muncie-Indianapolis & return.	"	" 423			
17	"	Indianapolis-Muncie & return.	"	" "		02	10
18	"	Richmond-Muncie & return.	"	" "			
18	"	Terre Haute - Effingham & return	"	" "		02	20
19	"	Local	"	" 449		01	05
20	"	"	"	" 228		01	—
20	"	"	"	" 234		01	—
21	"	"	"	" 416		03	—
21	"	Muncie-Lafayette Danville & return	"	" 428			
21	"	Evansville - Louisville & return.	"	" "			
						62	25

THE RECORD ON THIS PAGE IS CERTIFIED TRUE AND CORRECT:

PILOT Robert C. Sage ATTESTED BY

CARRY TOTALS FORWARD TO TOP OF NEXT PAGE

BREAKDOWN OF TRIP TIME INTO CLASSIFICATIONS												REMARKS
INSTRUMENT		~~INSTRUCTION~~ CO-PILOT		DAY		NIGHT		DUAL		SOLO		INSTRUCTOR SHOULD ENTER IN THIS COLUMN THE NATURE OF EACH MANEUVER IN WHICH INSTRUCTION IS GIVEN, AND THE TIME SPENT THEREON, AND SHALL ATTEST EACH SUCH ENTRY WITH HIS INITIALS, PILOT CERTIFICATE NUMBER, AND PERTINENT RATING.
15	30	31	50	41	40	09	10	21	45	29	05	
						01	—			01	—	T.
		01	50									Night Nav. X-C
						02	10			02	10	Nav. X-C.
		02	—									Nav. Night. X-C.
						02	20			02	20	Nav. X-C.
01	—	0	40	01	05					01	05	0:05 T.
		01	—			01	—			01	—	T.
		01	—			01	—			01	—	T.
						03	—	03	—			02:00 Formation — 01:00 Navigation.
		02	35									X-C. Nav.
		02	20									X-C. Nav.
16	30	43	15	42	45	19	40	24	45	37	40	ENTER IN THIS COLUMN DETAILS OF ANY SERIOUS DAMAGE TO AIRCRAFT. IF MORE SPACE THAN THAT PROVIDED ABOVE IS NEEDED FOR ANY DETAILS OF FLIGHT INSTRUCTION OR AIRCRAFT DAMAGE, USE PAGES PROVIDED IN BACK OF BOOK.
CARRY TOTALS FORWARD TO TOP OF NEXT PAGE												

DATE 1943	FLIGHT FROM	FLIGHT TO	AIRCRAFT MAKE AND MODEL	AIRCRAFT CERTIFICATE MARK	CLASSIFICATION			DURATION OF FLIGHT	
								62	25
22	Seymour, Ind.	Louisville, Ky. & return.	Beechcraft AT-10	Army-428					
22	"	Local	"	" 223				01	35
23	"	"	"	" 206				01	25
24	"	Effingham - Ind. and return.	"	" 415					
24	"	Local	"	" 425				0	35
25	"	Lafayette - Danville - Waterloo & return.	"	" 247				01	25
27	"	Local	"	" 234				01	35
28	"	Ft. Wayne - Richmond & return	"	" 426				01	55
Dec. 1	"	Local	"	" 415				01	—
2	"	"	"	" 426				02	—
THE RECORD ON THIS PAGE IS CERTIFIED TRUE AND CORRECT:								73	55
PILOT Robert C. Sage ATTESTED BY					CARRY TOTALS FORWARD TO TOP OF NEXT PAGE				

BREAKDOWN OF TRIP TIME INTO CLASSIFICATIONS

INSTRUMENT		~~INSTRUCTION~~ CO-PILOT		DAY		NIGHT		DUAL		SOLO		REMARKS INSTRUCTOR SHOULD ENTER IN THIS COLUMN THE NATURE OF EACH MANEUVER IN WHICH INSTRUCTION IS GIVEN, AND THE TIME SPENT THEREON, AND SHALL ATTEST EACH SUCH ENTRY WITH HIS INITIALS, PILOT CERTIFICATE NUMBER, AND PERTINENT RATING.
16	30	43	15	42	45	19	40	24	45	37	40	
		01	30									X-C-Nav. Rt engine cut out. Oil pressure.
01	30			01	35			01	35			0:05 T. Lt. Dickerhoof.
01	20			01	25			01	25			0:05 T. Lt. Dickerhoof.
		02	50									X-C-Nav. Night.
		02	15			0	35			0	35	T.
		01	25			01	25			01	25	X-C. Nav. Strange field landing. (Passed)
01	30			01	35			01	35			0:05 T. Instr. check. (50-3) Lt. C. Cavanagh
		01	—	01	55					01	55	X-C. Nav.
		01	—	01	—					01	—	Formation.
				02	—			02	—			Formation: Lt. R. S. Stainton
20	50	53	15	52	15	21	40	31	20	42	35	ENTER IN THIS COLUMN DETAILS OF ANY SERIOUS DAMAGE TO AIRCRAFT. IF MORE SPACE THAN THAT PROVIDED ABOVE IS NEEDED FOR ANY DETAILS OF FLIGHT INSTRUCTION OR AIRCRAFT DAMAGE, USE PAGES PROVIDED IN BACK OF BOOK.

CARRY TOTALS FORWARD TO TOP OF NEXT PAGE

Appendix B: List of Missions Flown[1]

[1] From RCS Diary, Thurleigh, U. K., 1944. 367th Bomb Squadron (The Clay Pigeons), 306th Heavy Bombardment Group. Specific targets for June 4 and 6, and for July 17, were added later by the author.

Date	Group No.	My No.	Target	Combat Hours
May 8	151	1	Berlin, Ger.	8:40
May 9	--	--	(Spare)	3:30
May 10	--	--	(Abandon)	3:45
May 11	--	--	(Spare)	3:20
May 12	154	2	Merseburg, Ger.	8:25
May 13	155	3	Stettin, Ger. (Poland)	10:45
May 22	158	4	Kiel, Ger.	7:45
May 23	159	5	Metz, Fr.	6:30
May 25	--	--	(Spare)	4:00
May 28	164	6	Ruhland, Ger.	8:30
May 31	166	7	Liege, Belgium	6:15
June 2	168	8	Massy-Paliseau, Fr.	5:50
June 4	170	9	Special Target, Fr. (Equihen)	4:30
June 6	171	10	(A) Special Target, Fr. (Arromanches)	5:55
June 6	173	11	(C) Special Target, Fr. (Thury-Harcourt)	5:20
June 12	--	--	(Spare)	4:15
June 15	178	12	Nantes, Fr.	6:40
June 17	179	13	Noyen, Fr.	6:35
June 18	180	14	Hamburg, Germany	7:45
June 19	181	15	Noball target, France	4:55
June 20	182	16	Hamburg, Germany	8:10
June 21	183	17	Berlin, Germany	10:20
June 22	184	18	Ghent, Belgium	5:15
June 24	185	19	Bremen, Germany	7:50
June 25	186	20	Joigny, France	6:30
July 17	197	21	Ham, France (St. Quentin/Jassy)	6:05
July 18	198	22	Peenemunde, Germany	9:20
July 20	200	23	Koethen, Germany	8:25
July 24	203	24	St. Lo, Normandy Front	5:20
July 25	204	25	St. Lo, Normandy Front	5:20
July 31	206	26	Munich, Germany	9:40
August 12	214	27	Chament, France	7:40
August 13	215	28	Rouen, (area), France	5:20
August 24		29	Merseburg, Germany	9:30

Appendix C: Selected Entries from the Squadron Diary, 367th Bombardment Squadron (H), 1944

THURY-HARCOURT - This group dispatched 36 a/c to form the 40th B CBW. Our squadron flew all positions of the lead squadron, lead group, except the lead a/c. Lt. Talmadge G. McDonough of our squadron led the high element of the high group. Our target was the lines of communication in the town of Thury-Harcourt. The assembly was made under the most adverse weather conditions and all the 306th planes never made this join up. The high group never found the lead and low groups and went on to bomb with planes from other fields. The lead and low groups were never completed, and even so some of the positions were filled by a/c from other bases. The target was bombed PFF with unobserved results by the lead and low groups. Lt. McDonough bombed with the high group, lead squadron, PFF, with unobserved results.

No flak or enemy a/c were seen, and all of our planes returned safely. On this mission there were clear areas and the crews reported seeing a great many fires on land. The sea was said to be filled with ships and landing craft. Other 367th pilots were: Lts. Joseph W. Pedersen, William M. Wood, Edward J. Magner, Williams H. McNeil and Virgil W. Dingman.

BERLIN - The 306th flew 54 a/c as the complete 40th A CBW. Our squadron flew planes in all three groups: Lts. William M. Wood, Joseph P. Couris and Charles C. Wegener flying #4, 5 and 6 positions of the lead group, high squadron; Lts. George J. Mapes, Daniel L. Speelman, Milton M. Adam and Charles M. Tell flying in the #2, 4, 5 and 6 positions of the high squadron, high group; Lt. Perry E. Raster led the low group with Lts. W. Bradley Butterfield, Williams H. McNeil, William R. Allen, Talmadge G. McDonough and Harold W. Barrett filling in the high squadron. The assembly was good and the northern route taken to the target, attacking from the East. Heavy clouds obscured the North Sea, but broke to generally clear before the target was reached. The bombing was visual, but dense contrails made it very difficult to pick up the aiming point and obscured the view at the time of bomb strikes. Photos locate some hits near Templehof A/D. Just before the target was reached Lt. Tell's a/c was straggling behind the formation a bit and was attacked by two FW 190s from 6 o'clock above. The tail and top turret both shot at him. Top turret's glass was hit by 20 mm and broken; the gunner, Sgt. Bernard E. Humiston, was uninjured and recovered to frame the E/A in his sights for a long burst. The FW nosed up and went into a dive, smoking, and then with flame pouring from it. At about 800 yards from 10 o'clock the enemy completely blew up. There was no other a/c in a position to fire on this fighter at the time. Sgt. Humiston has been awarded the Air Medal for a "destroyed". After this attack, Lt. Tell's left wing caught on fire, burned for some three to four minutes but went out. No members of the crew were injured. Tell was forced to land on a flat tire upon reaching base. Flak was very intense at the target and 26 a/c from the group were damaged. Lt. Adam of our squadron lost an engine over Berlin and then extinguished two external wing fires, before returning alone. He was covered by P-38s in the area and landed at Rackheath. This was a tough mission and we were fortunate in having all of our crews return.

ST. LO AREA - Today we sent the same force to the St. Lo area to repeat yesterday's performance of softening up the German lines for our ground forces. Today our squadron flew the 40th B-4 force, led by Lt. Joseph P. Couris. Lt. Paul F. Bailey flew with the 40th C-4 force. The weather was not as good as briefed but by dropping to 12,000 feet the bombardiers were able to locate their targets and drop with good results. Our squadron's bombs were dropped late to avoid dropping on another group that slid under our formation at the time when bombs should have been away. Photos show our strikes about one mile north of Marigny. On this mission the MPI was not a matter of hit or miss, but merely a means of distribution and our bombing was in all probability just as effective as if they had been placed right on the money. No E/A were encountered, nor any flak, and all A/c returned safely. Pilots for the 367th were: Lts. Charles M. Tell, Marion Plumb, Charles C. Wegener, John P. Heraty, Gordon L. Donkin, Milton M. Adam, Williams H. McNeil, Frank A. Wagenfohr, George J. Mapes, Robert C. Sage and Harold W. Barrett.

MERSEBERG - The 306th flew the complete 40th A CBW. Our squadron flew the lead squadron and the low element of the high group. Lt. Talmadge G. McDonough led. Lt. Frank A. Wagenfohr was designated as spare for this group and filled in for F/O Robert D. Stewart in the high element when Stewart was forced to abort due to mechanical failure. The route was flown over an 8/10ths undercast

BOHLEN - 35 a/c of the 306th flew the 40th B CBW to bomb the synthetic oil plant at Bohlen, Germany. Our squadron flew nine a/c in the lead group. Lt. Gordon L. Donkin flew with Maj. Maurice Salada, 368th C.O., in the lead a/c. When the formation reached the target it was covered by smoke from previous bombing, and a new MPI was selected and hit. High group was slightly over, and the low group bombed into smoke. Flak at the target was very intense and extremely accurate. The 369th lost two a/c and of the 33 returning to base, 31 were damaged. Every plane from our squadron, except one, was hit. Our only injuries were two men who received slight cuts from flying plexiglas. No fighters attacked our CBW, but the wing ahead was seen to be under attack. The weather was good during the entire mission with only a high cirrus at 30,000 feet that disappeared over the target. Other pilots for the 367th were: Lts. Richard H. Metzger, Frank A. Wagenfohr, John P. Heraty, Eldon J. Burrell, Harold W. Barrett, Lewis H. White, Paul F. Bailey and John K. McAllister.

MERSEBERG and VORDEN A/D - The 306th put up 36 a/c as the 40th C CBW. Our squadron flew nine a/c as the three-ship high elements of each group. The target was the synthetic oil works at Merseberg, Germany. Lead and high groups bombed very successfully on the main plant. The group was interfered with on the bomb run and did not drop. Later they made a run on the Vorden A/D northeast of Kassel. Our pictures show hits on the dispersal area. Flak at the target was very accurate, and our formation came a bit too close to Leipzig and got flak from there also. All except one of our a/c were damaged; however, no personnel were injured. Our fighter support was scattered and not too good; fortunately, no E/A were seen. Pilots for the 367th were: Lts. Robert C. Sage, John K. McAllister, Richard H. Metzger, Harold W. Barrett, Paul F. Bailey, Eldon J. Burrell, Milton M. Adam, Irving B. Pedersen, and Robert L. Cardon.

PEENEMUNDE, GERMANY - 36 a/c of the 306th flew the 40th A CBW to

Appendix D: Selected Interrogation Forms, Intelligence Narrative, Track Charts, and Flight Diagrams Pertaining to the 367th B.S. and the RCS Diary

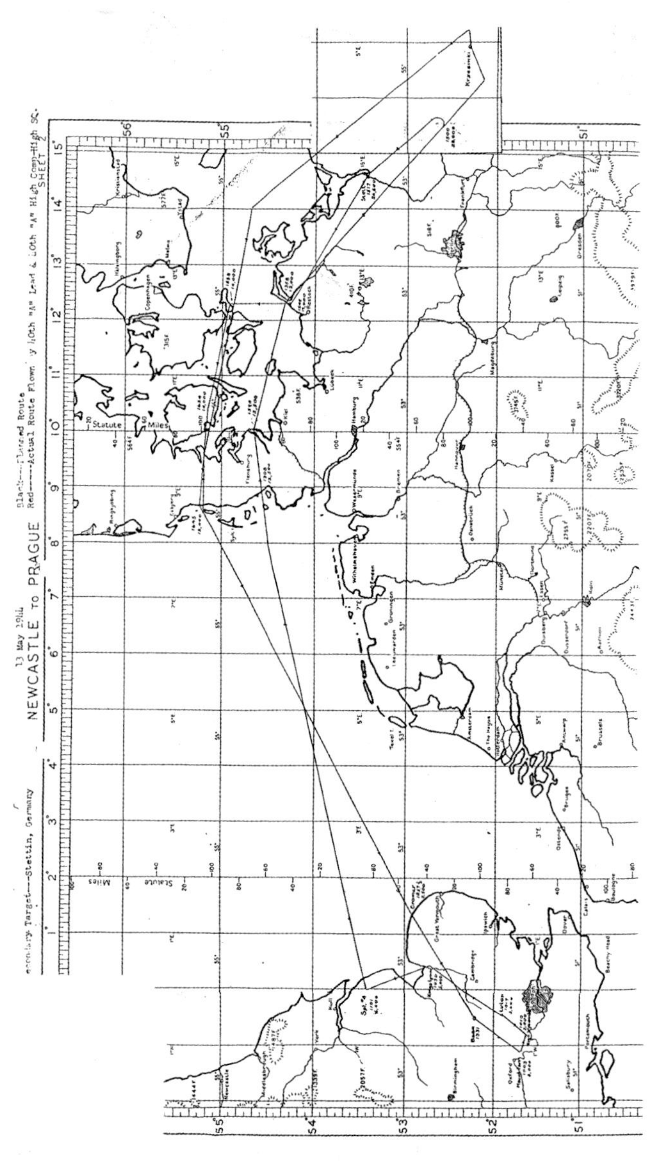

---- MISSION LOADING LIST ----

SQUADRON 367th MISSION NUMBER 155 DATE May 13, 1944.

A/C Number 42-31726
Total time for complete mission 10:55

(P)	PETERS,	B.H.	1st Lt.
(CP)	PITBLADO,	W.J.	1st Lt.
(N)	GUSTAFSON,	R.E.	1st Lt.
(B)	LEGOWSKI,	H.R.	1st Lt.
(E)	Hoffman,	K.E.	T/Sgt.
✓ (R)	Hill,	T.R.	T/Sgt.
✓ (G)	Raymond,	C.W.	S/Sgt.
✓ (G)	Downs,	S.G.	S/Sgt.
✓ (G)	Tricoglov,	J.D.	S/Sgt.
(G)			
( )			

A/C Number 42-97278
Total time for complete mission 10:45

(P)	MC DONOUGH,	T.G.	2nd Lt.
(CP)	SAGE,	R.C.	2nd Lt.
(N)	CRUNICAN,	C.J.	2nd Lt.
(B)	CARELLA,	J.M.	1st Lt.
(E)	Carter,	D.M.	S/Sgt.
✓ (RO)	Malan,	E.A.	S/Sgt.
✓ (G)	Weeter,	R.E.	Sgt.
✓ (G)	Shaw,	R.W.	Sgt.
✓ (G)	Vaughan,	W.R.	Cpl.
(G)			
( )			

A/C Number 42-297312
Total time for Complete mission 10:25

(P)	PEDERSEN,	J.W.	2nd Lt.
(CP)	BLOOD,	L.J.	2nd Lt.
(N)	EILAR,	N.W.	2nd Lt.
(B)	SMITH,	W.A.	1st Lt.
(E)	Arnold,	B.F.	S/Sgt.
✓ (RO)	Wonning,	J.E.	S/Sgt.
✓ (G)	Blackwell,	J.E.	Sgt.
✓ (G)	Kerr,	W.E.	Sgt.
✓ (G)	Ehrhard,	H.P.	Sgt.
(G)			
( )			

A/C Number 42-107032
Total time for Complete mission 10:00

(P)	HANSON,	H.E.	1st Lt.
(CP)	LOCKE,	E.W.	2nd Lt.
(N)	KIELY,	V.J.	2nd Lt.
(B)	CLEMENTS,	G.W.	2nd Lt.
(E)	Maxwell,	R.L.	T/Sgt.
✓ (RO)	O'Malley,	C.A.	S/Sgt.
✓ (G)	Urban,	D.F.	S/Sgt.
✓ (G)	Hamilton,	J.T.	S/Sgt.
✓ (G)	Bloise,	D.M.	S/Sgt.
(G)			
( )			

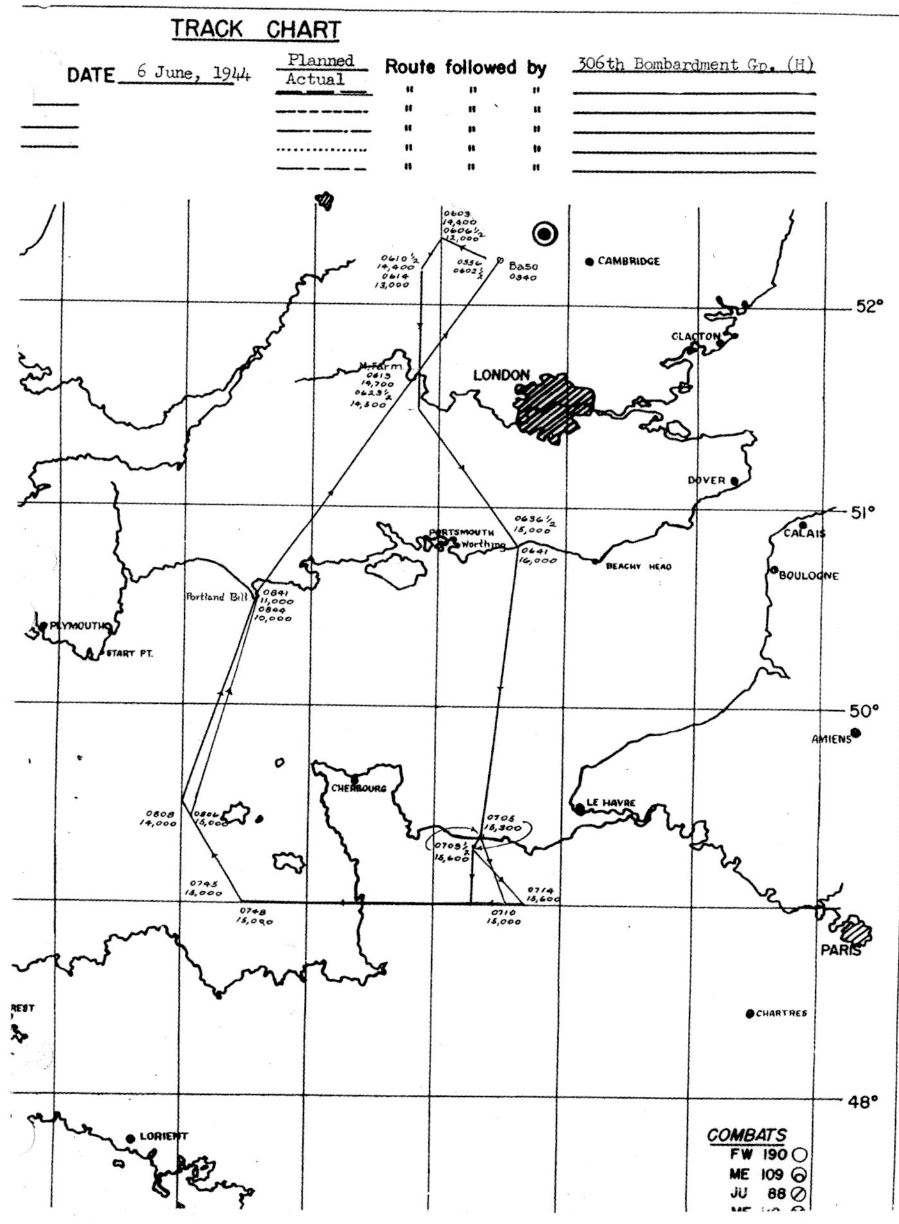
TRACK CHART
DATE 6 June, 1944
Planned
Actual
Route followed by 306th Bombardment Gp. (H)
Base
CAMBRIDGE
CLACTON
LONDON
DOVER
PORTSMOUTH
Worthing
BEACHY HEAD
CALAIS
BOULOGNE
Portland Bill
PLYMOUTH
START PT.
AMIENS
CHERBOURG
LE HAVRE
PARIS
CHARTRES
LORIENT
52°
51°
50°
48°
COMBATS
FW 190
ME 109
JU 88

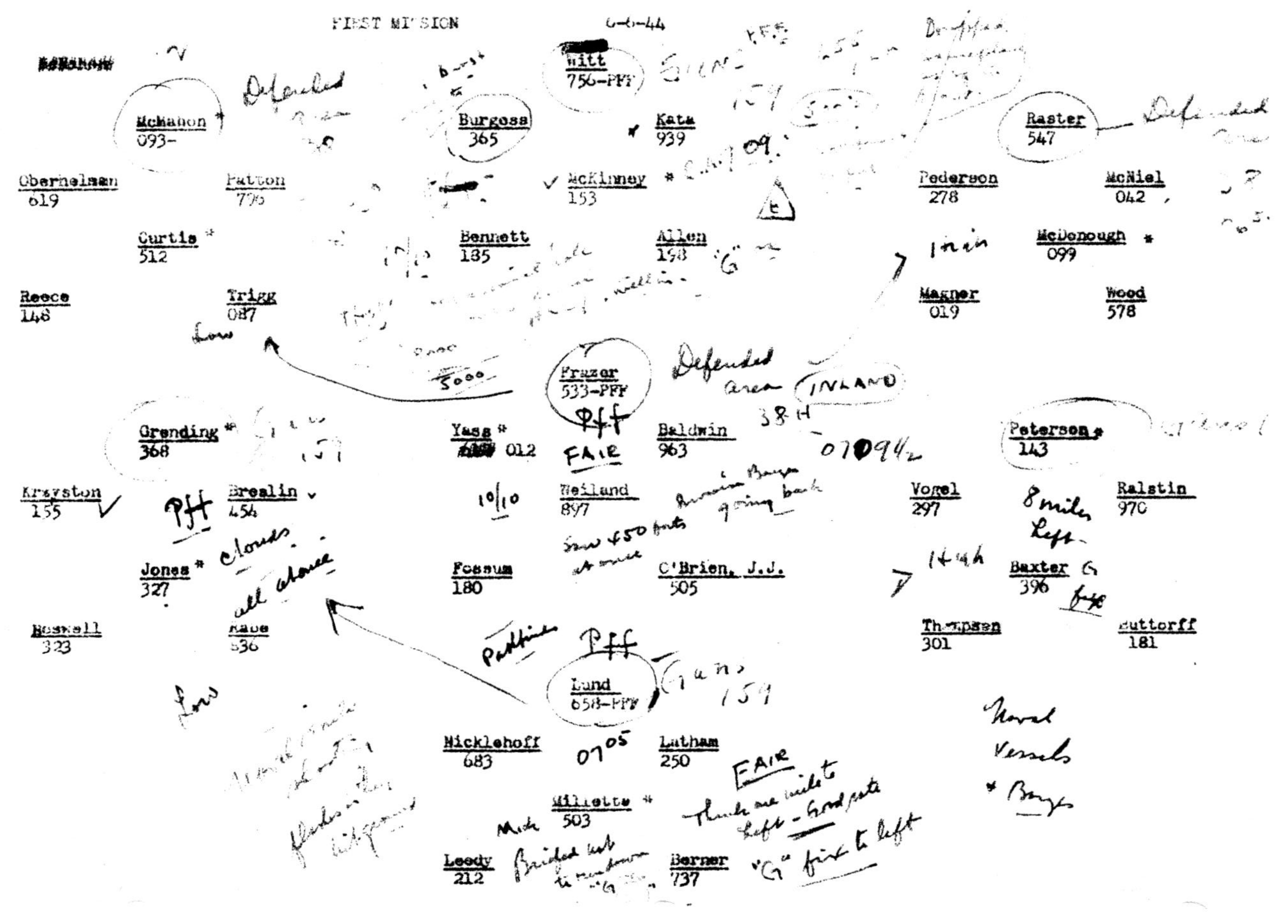

FIRST MISSION 6-6-44

Witt 756-PFF

McMahon 093- Burgess 365 Kats 939 Raster 547

Obernelman 019 Patton 776 McKinney 153 Pederson 278 McNiel 042

Curtis * 512 Bennett 135 Allen 198 McDonough * 099

Reece 148 Trigg 087 Wagner 019 Wood 578

Frazer 533-PFF

Grending * 368 Yass * 012 Baldwin 963 Peterson * 143

Kreyston 155 Breslin 454 Weiland 897 Vogel 297 Ralstin 970

Jones * 327 Fossum 180 O'Brien, J.J. 505 Baxter 396

Boswell 323 Kase 536 Thompson 301 Guttorff 181

Lund 658-PFF

Micklehoff 683 Latham 250

Millette * 503

Leedy 212 Berner 737

INTERROGATION FORM

SQUADRON 367 A/C Number 099 Letter S Date 6 June, 1944

Bomb Load 38 x 100, G.P.

Time Took off 0440 Time Landed 1018

Position in Formation

Rastin's Sqd

1. HOT NEWS to be phoned in? Yes No
   Details:

Friendly A/C in any kind of distress: (Give position, time, altitude, full details)

CREW: Give Rank and Initials

2nd Lt. T.G. McDonough	Pilot
2nd Lt. R.C. Sage	Co-P
2nd Lt. E.L. Ronczy	Nav.
2nd Lt. C.J. Crunican	Bomb
T/Sgt. E.A. Malan.	Radio
T/Sgt. D.M. Carter	Top T
S/Sgt. R.W. Shaw	Ball T
S/Sgt. E.F. Dickhaus	R. Waist
	L. Waist
S/Sgt. F.B. Lauer	Tail G.

2. TARGET ATTACKED:

Primary Time: 0709.1

Alternate Height: 15,800

Last Report Reading: 218 mag
(circle)

Duration Bomb Run:

3. Number of BOMBS dropped on target: All Jettisoned: Returned: Abortive:

4. Observed RESULTS OF BOMBING: (For this plane or others)

Own Bombs: ✓

Other Bombing:

Any Nickels: Yes No
Number boxes dropped
Number Boxes returned

5. Any PHOTOGRAPHS taken: (Yes?) No?

6. GROUND TARGETS ATTACKED BY GUNFIRE AND RESULTS:

7. ROUTE (If different than ordered) (If ABORTIVE give time, place, height of turn; reason for returning early, and Disposition of bombs.) ✓

8. WEATHER: (If it affected mission) ✓

9. FLAK: Encountered on way out, at target and on way home.

Time	Place	Height of A/C	Type (light, heavy), intense,	Color of	Location Bursts in re-	Accurac;

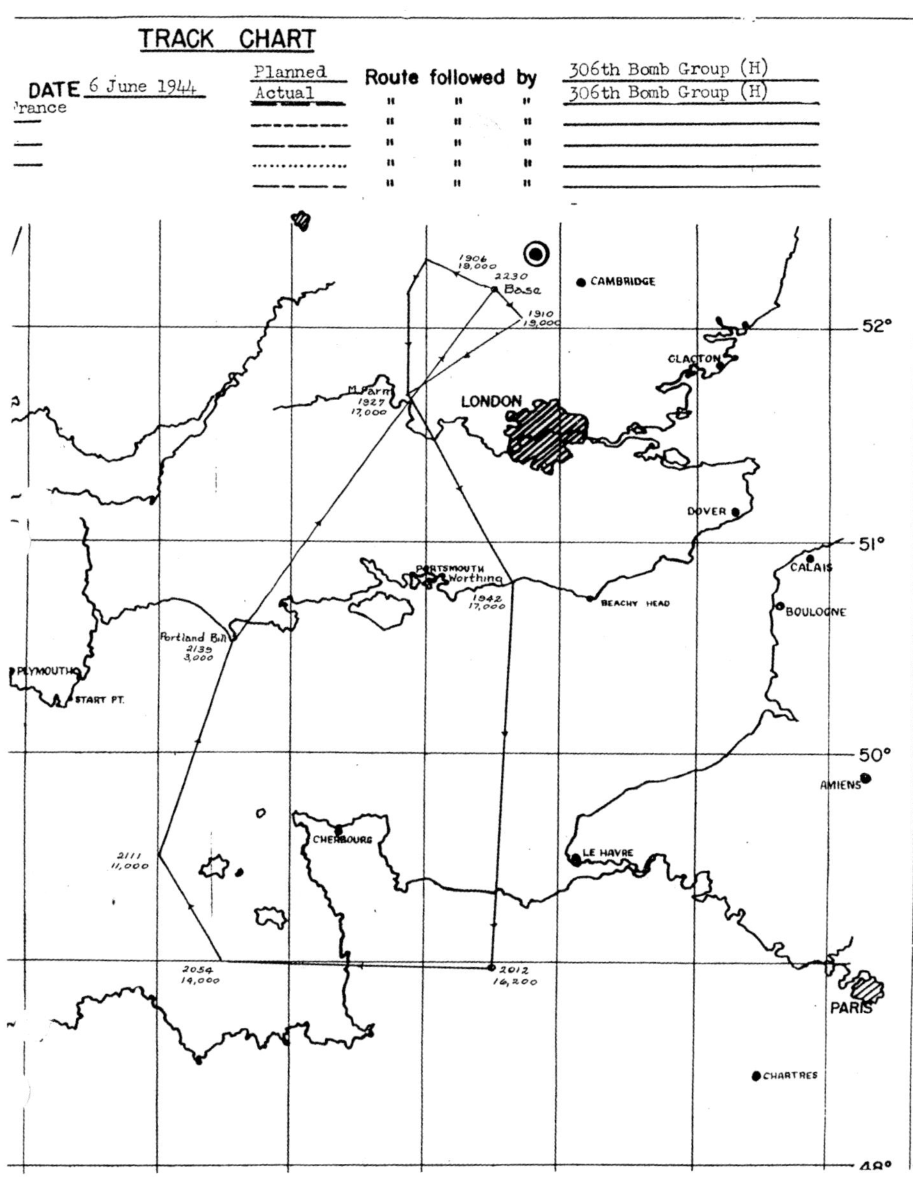
TRACK CHART
DATE 6 June 1944
'rance
Planned
Actual
Route followed by
306th Bomb Group (H)
306th Bomb Group (H)
1906
18,000
2230
Base
1910
19,000
CAMBRIDGE
52°
CLACTON
M.Farm
1927
17,000
LONDON
DOVER
51°
PORTSMOUTH
Worthing
1942
17,000
CALAIS
BEACHY HEAD
BOULOGNE
Portland Bill
2139
3,000
PLYMOUTH
START PT.
50°
AMIENS
CHERBOURG
2111
11,000
LE HAVRE
2054
14,000
2012
16,200
PARIS
CHARTRES
48°

INTERROGATION FORM

SQUADRON 367 A/C Number: 099 Letter S Date 6/6/4

Bomb Load 12x500 H.E. Incend.

Time Took off 1754 Time Landed 2248

Position in Formation

HIGH

Alone Head in PFF

1. HOT NEWS to be phoned in? Yes No
Details:

Friendly A/C in any kind of distress: (Give position, time, altitude, full details)

CREW: Give Rank and Initials

2/Lt. MC DONOUGH, T.D.	Pilot
2/Lt. SAGE, R.C.	Co-P
2/Lt. RONCZY, E.L.	Nav.
2/Lt. CRUNIGAN, C.J.	Bomb
T/SGT. CARTER, D.M.	Radio
T/SGT. MALAN, E.A.	Top T
S/SGT. SHAW, R.W.	Ball T
S/SGT. DICKHAUS, E.F.	R. Waist
	L. Waist
S/SGT. LAUER, F.B.	Tail G.

2. TARGET ATTACKED:

Primary Time: 2012

Alternate Height: 17200

Last Report (circle) Heading: 244

Duration Bomb Run:

Dropped on PFF ship -

3. Number of BOMBS dropped on target: All Jettisoned: Returned: Abortive:

4. Observed RESULTS OF BOMBING: (For this plane or others)

Own Bombs: Clouds there - could not quite identify -

Other Bombing: But

Any Nickels: Yes No
Number Boxes dropped
Number Boxes returned

5. Any PHOTOGRAPHS taken: Yes? No?

6. GROUND TARGETS ATTACKED BY GUNFIRE AND RESULTS:

7. ROUTE (If different than ordered) (If ABORTIVE give time, place, height of turn; reason for returning early, and Disposition of bombs.)

This A/C + PFF Ship (7565) XK went in alone and came out alone - Saw other formations but not ours - Went in as briefed but too far left on target run - Feel we were ahead - at 12 wove thru Clouds giving trouble at Rendezvous. Finally found our wing PFF ship at 2105 and proceeded.

8. WEATHER: (If it affected mission)

9. FLAK: Encountered on way out, at target and on way home.

Time	Place	Height of A/C	Type (light, heavy), intense, moderate or	Color of Bursts	Location Bursts in relation to A/C	Accuracy

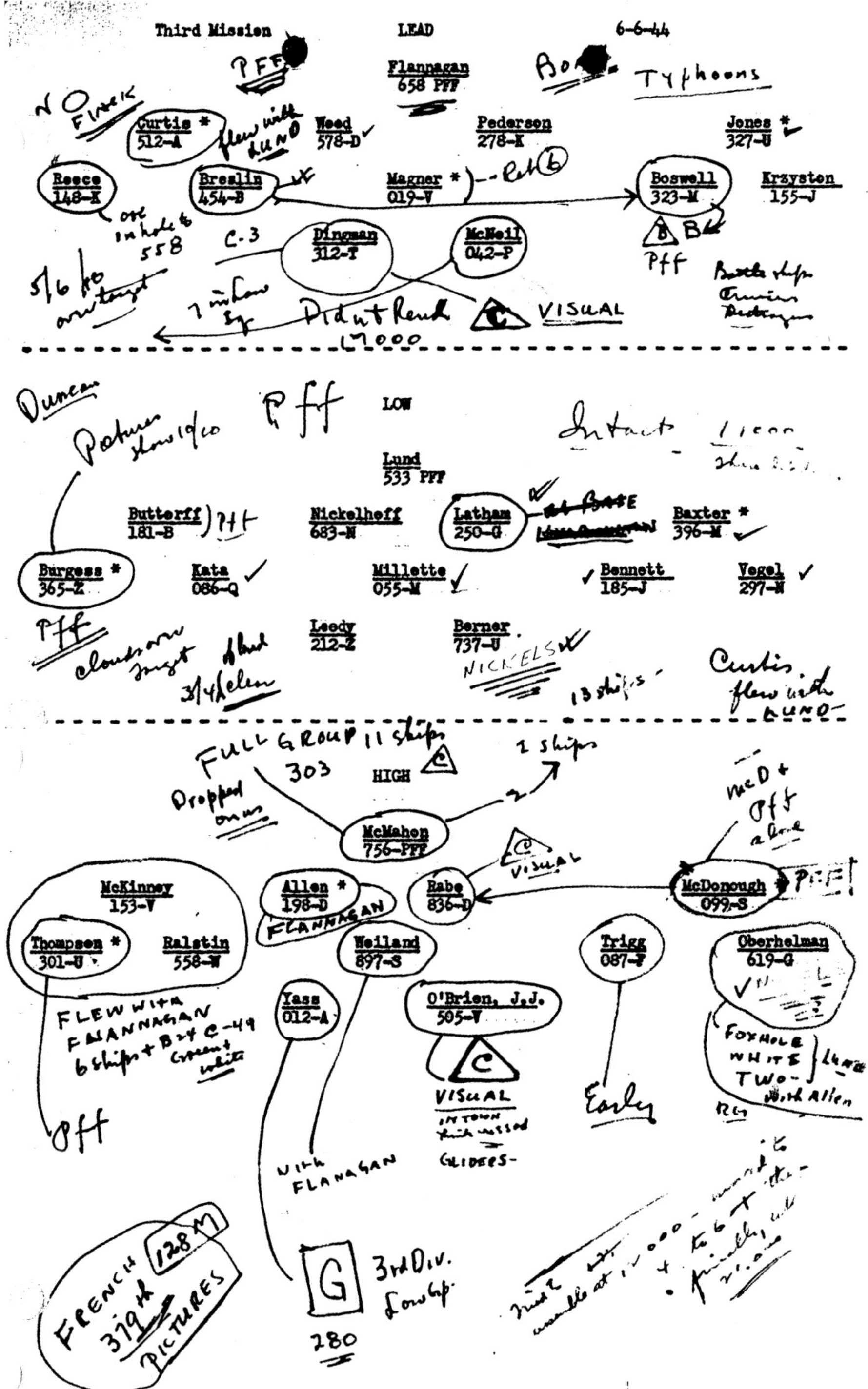

Third Mission LEAD 6-6-44

PFF

Flannagan 658 PFF

Typhoons

NO FLAK

Curtis * 512-A — flew with LUND

Weed 578-D

Pederson 278-K

Jones * 327-U

Reece 148-K

Breslin 454-B

Magner * 019-V

Boswell 323-M

Krzyston 155-J

C-3

Dingman 312-T

McNeil 042-P

PFF

VISUAL

17000

Duncan

PFF

LOW

Lund 533 PFF

Intacts

Butterfi 181-B

Nickelhoff 683-N

Latham 250-G

Baxter * 396-M

Burgess * 365-Z

Kata 086-Q

Millette 055-M

Bennett 185-J

Vogel 297-N

PFF

Leedy 212-Z

Berner 737-U

NICKELS

13 ships

Curtis flew with LUND

FULL GROUP 11 ships

303

HIGH

2 ships

Dropped ours

McMahon 756-PFF

McD + PFF alone

VISUAL

McKinney 153-V

Allen * 198-D — FLANNAGAN

Rabe 836-D

McDonough 099-S — PFF

Thompson * 301-U

Ralstin 558-W

Weiland 897-S

Trigg 087-F

Oberhelman 619-G

FLEW WITH FLANNAGAN 6 ships + B24 C-49

Yass 012-A

O'Brien, J.J. 505-V

FOXHOLE WHITE TWO — with Allen

VISUAL

IN TOWN

GLIDERS-

Early

PFF

WITH FLANAGAN

G 3rd Div.

280

FRENCH 128 M 379th PICTURES

OPERATIONAL REPORT IVR20 V-318D

NARRATIVE SECTION
"B"

PRIORITY
TO: C.G., 1st Bomb Division,
40th Combat Wing,
Attention: A-2.

XXXXXXX

1. A/C 144-J, pilot Johnson, dropped 10 G44's over Hamburg.

2. Photos show 306th Lead Group XXXXX bombs on marshalling yard directly east of target. Low Group hit MPI, High Group hit almost on top, extending pattern to West. Photos show tremendous column of black smoke from 1633A and probably B. Oil fire from 1622E and 1630.

3. XXXXXXXXX No attacks were made on this group. 1 crew reported seeing 2 Me 410s shot down by 51's and 38's in target area. P-38s were picked up late at 0900 hours at 5405N x 1040E, possibly because this CBW was 10 minutes ahead of time. Support always present thereafter. 38s through target, 51s in target area, 47s from there out.

4. A moderate to intense barrage observed to right while on bomb run. The biggest concentration of guns appeared to be located to the east of the lake. Intense accurate tracking fire damaged lead and high groups severely but was inaccurate on low group. 9 slight , two severe, Lead Group. Two slight, Low Group. 1 A/C direct hit, 5 severe, 7 slight, high Group.

5. 10/10ths undercast over North Sea to four degrees east. 5/10ths to 8 degrees east. Clear over target.

6. Very thick smoke screen observed at Hamburg as formation passed over Danish Peninsula, not operating on bomb run. Smoke screens also observed at Kiel, Bremen, Wilhelmshaven, Lubeck, Lutzenburg.
25 to 30 T/E A/C at Nordholz A/D.
25 A/C on A/D at Heligoland.
20 A/C on A/D at Travemunde (5357N x 1052E)
20 to 30 A/C, some four-engine, at A/D at 5354N x 1128E.
Large column of white smoke from direction of Hanover, rising to estimated altitude of 20,000 feet.

7. Course
306th flew lead, low and high groups of 40 "B" CBW. After assembling as briefed, left English Coast at 0635. Due to change in winds, reached German Coast 10 minutes early at 0842, crossing slightly South of course at 5410N x 0850E to avoid flak at Westerhever. Returning to briefed course, reached target 15 minutes early at 0925. Shortly after leaving last control point over Germany, ~~at 5350N x 0833E~~ many groups of other CBW's converged, temporarily upsetting our Wing formation. Reforming, Wing crossed German Coast at 5350N x 0833E at 0946 and returned to base on briefed course, crossing the Wash at 1134, landing at 1207.

Aircraft in Distress

Our A/C 250-G, pilot Latham, hit by flak after bombs away. One to four chutes reported.

One B-17, from CBW behind, hit by flak over target, exploded before hitting ground. Most crews reported seeing no chutes. One reported seeing one chute and one reported 7 or 8 chutes out.

Messages were received from two B-24s saying they were going to ditch. Also heard Air Sea Rescue reply.

Message was received on VHF saying that a B-17 had 2 engines working and going down about 15 minutes off German coast. B-17's group leader advised going to Sweden and gave a heading to take. Time 1050 hours.

A message was received from A/C, call sign "WBUU", on "A" channel saying he was having difficulty at 1108 hours, position believed to be 5340N x 0040E. Complete message phoned to Division.

Aircraft Returning Early

A/C 148-K, pilot Reece, turned back at English Coast, ignition lead #3 engine broken. Brought back 12 x 500.

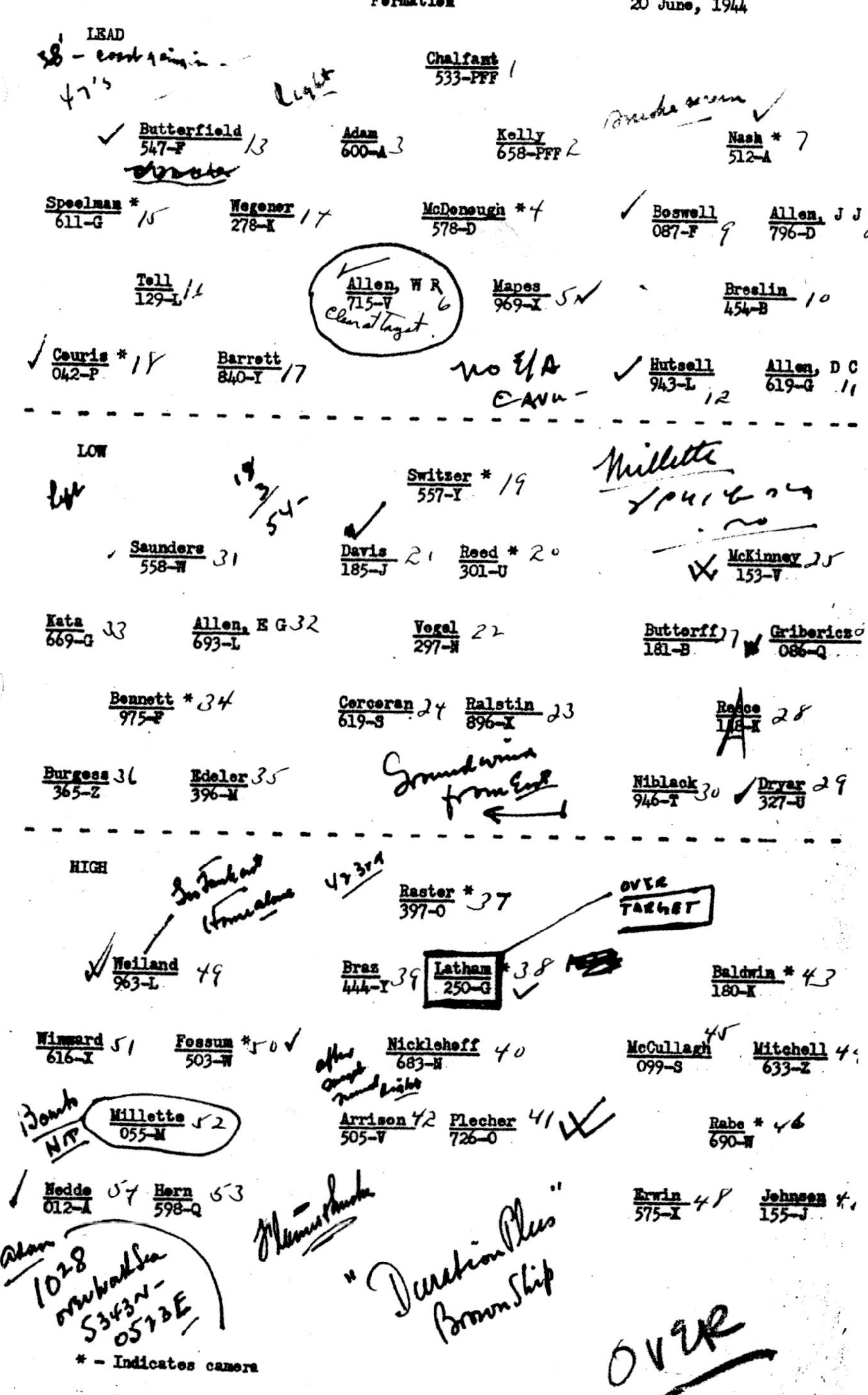

Formation 20 June, 1944

LEAD

Chalfant 533-PFF

Butterfield 547-F — Adam 600-A — Kelly 658-PFF — Nash * 512-A

Speelman * 611-G — Wegener 278-K — McDonough * 578-D — Boswell 087-F — Allen, J J 796-D

Tell 129-L — Allen, W R 715-V — Mapes 969-X — Breslin 454-B

Couris * 042-P — Barrett 840-Y — Hutsell 943-L — Allen, D C 619-G

- -

LOW

Switzer * 557-Y

Saunders 558-W — Davis 185-J — Reed * 301-U — McKinney 153-V

Kata 669-G — Allen, E G 693-L — Vogel 297-N — Butterff 181-B — Griberics 086-Q

Bennett * 975-F — Corcoran 619-S — Ralstin 896-X — Reece 118-K

Burgess 365-Z — Edeler 396-M — Niblack 946-T — Dryar 327-U

- -

HIGH

Raster * 397-O

Weiland 963-L — Braz 444-Y — Latham * 250-G — Baldwin * 180-K

Winmard 616-X — Fossum * 503-W — Nickleheff 683-N — McCullagh 099-S — Mitchell 633-Z

Millette 055-M — Arrison 505-V — Plecher 726-O — Rabe * 690-W

Hedde 012-A — Horn 598-Q — Erwin 575-X — Johnson 155-J

* - Indicates camera

"Duration Plus" Brown Ship

OVER

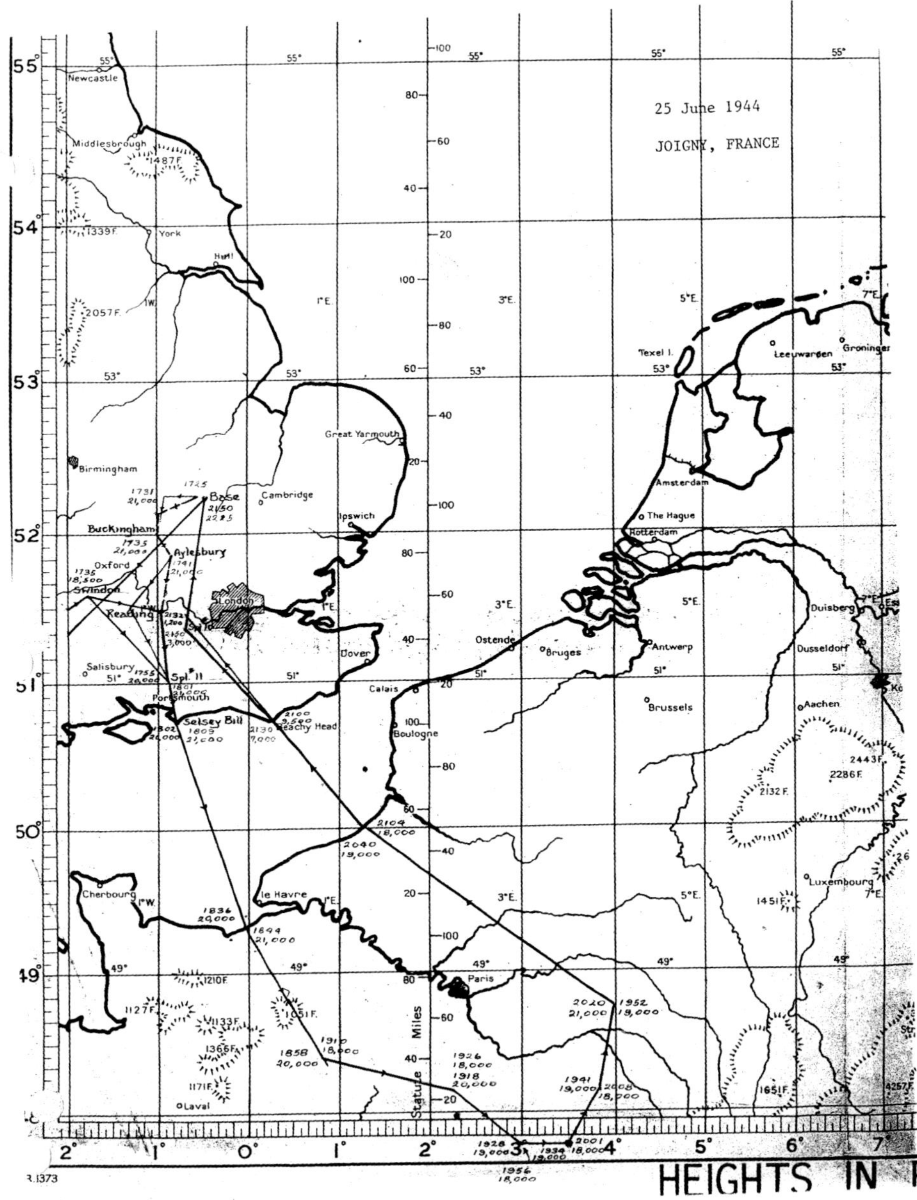

25 June 1944
JOIGNY, FRANCE
Newcastle
Middlesbrough
York
Hull
Birmingham
Cambridge
Ipswich
Great Yarmouth
Buckingham
Aylesbury
Oxford
Swindon
Reading
London
Salisbury
Portsmouth
Selsey Bill
Beachy Head
Dover
Calais
Boulogne
Cherbourg
le Havre
Paris
Laval
Ostende
Bruges
Antwerp
Brussels
Amsterdam
The Hague
Rotterdam
Texel I.
Leeuwarden
Groningen
Duisberg
Dusseldorf
Aachen
Luxembourg
Base
Statute Miles
HEIGHTS IN

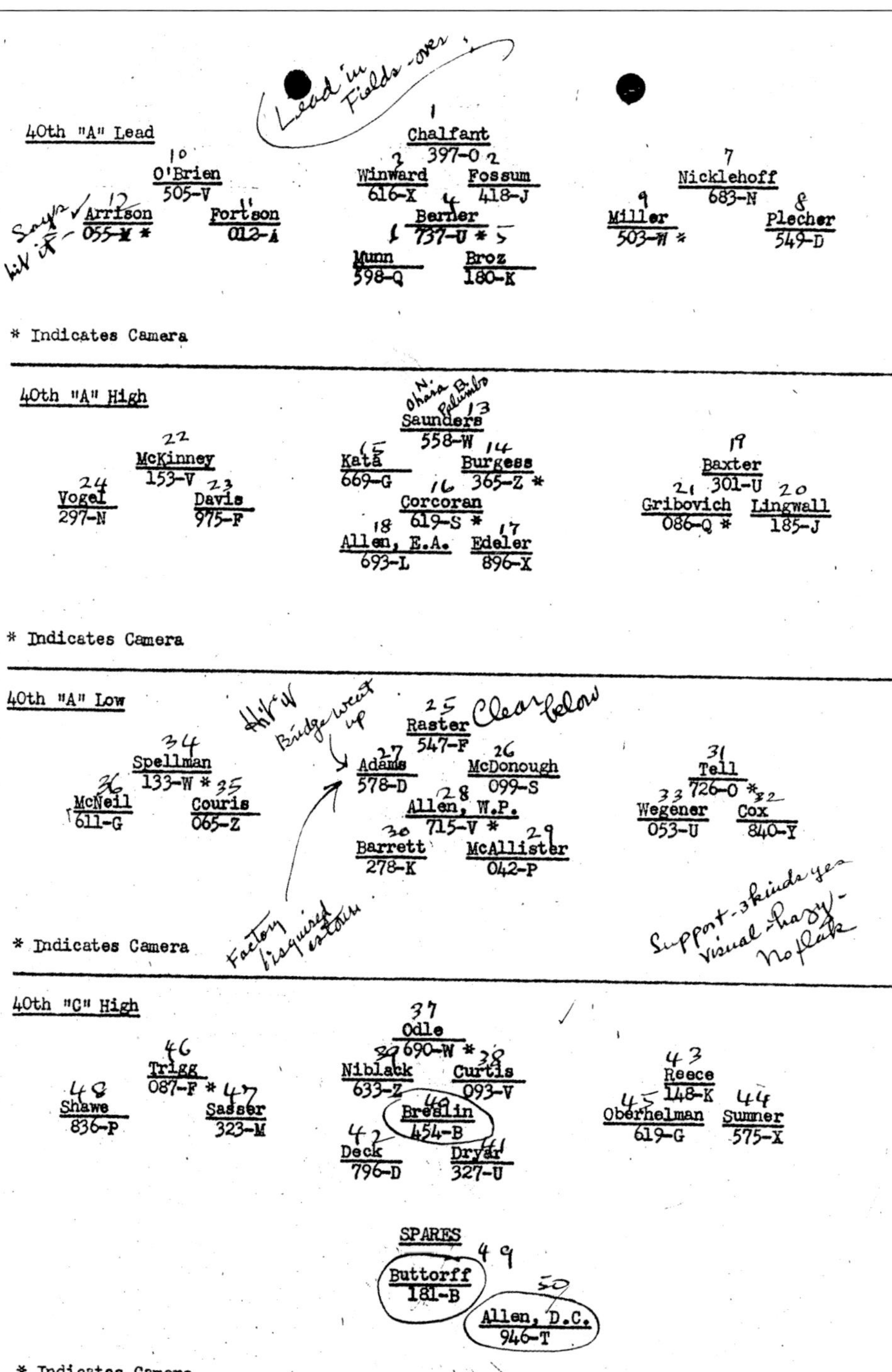

40th "A" Lead

Chalfant 397-O

O'Brien 505-V

Winward 616-X

Fossum 418-J

Nicklehoff 683-N

Arrison 055-M *

Fortson 012-A

Berner 737-U *

Miller 503-W *

Plecher 549-D

Munn 598-Q

Broz 180-K

* Indicates Camera

40th "A" High

Saunders 558-W

McKinney 153-V

Kata 669-G

Burgess 365-Z *

Baxter 301-U

Vogel 297-N

Davis 975-F

Corcoran 619-S *

Gribovich 086-Q *

Lingwall 185-J

Allen, E.A. 693-L

Edeler 896-X

* Indicates Camera

40th "A" Low

Raster 547-F

Spellman 133-W *

Adams 578-D

McDonough 099-S

Tell 726-O *

McNeil 611-G

Couris 065-Z

Allen, W.P. 715-V *

Wegener 053-U

Cox 840-Y

Barrett 278-K

McAllister 042-P

* Indicates Camera

40th "C" High

Odle 690-W *

Trigg 087-F *

Niblack 633-Z

Curtis 093-V

Reece 148-K

Shawe 836-P

Sasser 323-M

Breslin 454-B

Oberhelman 619-G

Sumner 575-X

Deck 796-D

Dryer 327-U

SPARES

Buttorff 181-B

Allen, D.C. 946-T

* Indicates Camera

26

INTERROGATION FORM

SQUADRON 367 A/C Number 099 Letter S Date 25 June 1944

Bomb Load 2 x 2000 H.E. Position in Formation 40 CBW "A" low

Time Took off 1552 Time Landed 2005

1. HOT NEWS to be phoned in? Yes No
   Details: —

CREW: Give Rank and Initials

1st Lt. McDonough T.	Pilot
2nd Lt. R.C. Sage	C.P
2nd Lt. E.L. Ronczy	Nav.
1st Lt. H.R. Maroney	Bomb
T/Sgt. E.A. Malan	Radio
T/Sgt. D.M. Carter	Top T
S/Sgt. R.W. Shaw	Ball T
S/Sgt. J.J. Robbins	R. Waist
	L. Waist
S/Sgt. P. Szymanski	Tail G.

Friendly A/C in any kind of distress: (Give position, time, altitude, full details)

2. TARGET ATTACKED:
   (Primary) Time: 1934½
   Alternate Height: 19000
   Last Resort Heading: 98°
   (circle)
   Function Bomb Run: 4 minutes

3. Number of BOMBS dropped on target: 2x2000 Jettisoned: Returned: Abortive:

4. Observed RESULTS OF BOMBING: (For this plane or others)

Own Bombs: on target.

Other Bombing:

Any Nickels: Yes No
Number Boxes dropped
Number Boxes returned

5. Any PHOTOGRAPHS taken: Yes? (No?)

6. GROUND TARGETS ATTACKED BY GUNFIRE AND RESULTS:

7. ROUTE (If different than ordered) (If ABORTIVE give time, place, height of turn, reason for returning early, and Disposition of bombs.) 21000

8. WEATHER: (If it affected mission) clear, 10/10 at coast breaking on way to target.

9. FLAK: Encountered on way out, at target and on way home.

Time	Place	Height of A/C	Type (light, heavy), intense, moderate or slight.	Color of Bursts	Location Bursts in relation to A/C	Accuracy

Troyes — obs.
49°40'N 03°00'E — obs. — [illegible]

Crew observations about Flak:

no chaff
very meager non persistent con trails

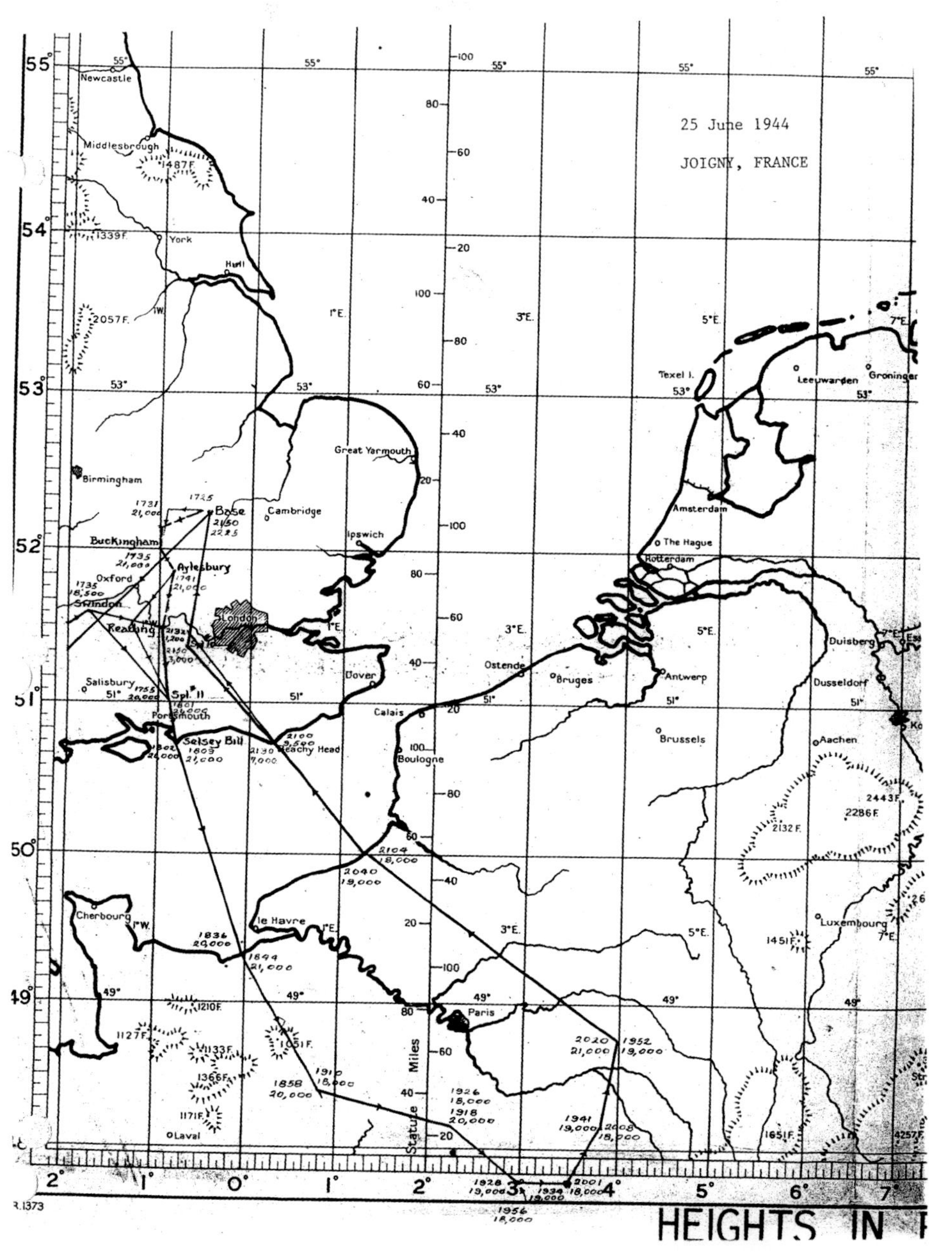

25 June 1944
JOIGNY, FRANCE
HEIGHTS IN F

INTERROGATION FORM 53

SQUADRON 367 ~~368XX369XXX423~~ A/C Number 065 Letter Z Date 24 July, 1944

Bomb Load 38 x 100 H.E. Incend.

Time Took Off 10:22 Time Landed ________

Position in Formation

X
X X X X
X X X X X
X X X (X) X 40 C-4
X X X X

1. HOT NEWS to be phoned in? Yes No
   Details:

   Friendly A/C in any kind of distress: (Give position, time, altitude, full details)

CREW: Give Rank and Initials

1st Lt. R. C. Sage	Pilot
2nd Lt. P. H. Martin	Co-P
1st Lt. E. L. Ronczy	Nav.
1st Lt. C. J. Crunican	Bomb
T/Sgt. M. J. Kilcoyne	Radio
T/Sgt. D. M. Carter	Top
S/Sgt. R. W. Shaw	Ball
S/Sgt. L. A. Ristuccia	R/W
[illegible]	L/W
S/Sgt. F. B. Lauer	Tail

2. TARGET ATTACKED:
   Primary Time: 1251½
   Alternate Height: 25,300
   Last Resort Heading: 219°
   (circle)
   Duration Bomb Run:

3. Number of BOMBS dropped on target: all Jettisoned: Returned: Abortive:

4. Observed RESULTS OF BOMBING: (For this plane or others)

   Own Bombs: Saw smoke and dropped past it.

   Other Bombing:

   Any Nickels: ____ Yes ____ No
   Number bombs dropped ________
   Number Bombs returned ________

5. Any PHOTOGRAPHS taken: Yes? No?

6. GROUND TARGETS ATTACKED BY GUNFIRE AND RESULTS:

7. ROUTE: (If different than ordered) (If ABORTIVE give time, place, height of turn; reason for returning early, and Disposition of bombs.)

   With Group

8. WEATHER: (If it affected mission)

9. FLAK: Encountered on way out, at target and on way home.

Time	Place	Height of A/C	Type (light heavy), intense, moderate or	Color of Bursts	Location Bursts in relation to A/C	Accuracy

Appendix E: Robert C. Sage Certification of Military Service and Report of Separation

SEPARATION FILE 8-17-45-9M

MILITARY RECORD AND REPORT OF SEPARATION
CERTIFICATE OF SERVICE C-4585-724

1. LAST NAME - FIRST NAME - MIDDLE INITIAL: SAGE ROBERT C
2. ARMY SERIAL NUMBER: 0-[illegible]
3. GRADE: 1ST LT
4. ARM OR SERVICE: AC
5. COMPONENT: AUS
6. ORGANIZATION: 1077TH ARMY AIR FORCE BASE UNIT SQUADRON E, BOWMAN FIELD, KENTUCKY
7. DATE OF RELIEF FROM ACTIVE DUTY: 22 JUNE 45
8. PLACE OF SEPARATION: SEPARATION CENTER FORT DIX, NEW JERSEY
9. PERMANENT ADDRESS FOR MAILING PURPOSES: 4830 CASTOR AVENUE, PHILADELPHIA, 24 PENNSYLVANIA
10. DATE OF BIRTH: 14 JUNE 21
11. PLACE OF BIRTH: PHILADELPHIA PENNSYLVANIA
12. ADDRESS FROM WHICH EMPLOYMENT WILL BE SOUGHT: SEE 9
13. COLOR EYES: BLUE
14. COLOR HAIR: BLONDE
15. HEIGHT: 72"
16. WEIGHT: 148 LBS.
17. NO. OF DEPENDENTS: 1
18. RACE: WHITE X
19. MARITAL STATUS: MARRIED X
20. U.S. CITIZEN: YES X
21. CIVILIAN OCCUPATION AND NO.: JUNIOR EXECUTIVE - 0-97.14

MILITARY HISTORY

22. SELECTIVE SERVICE DATA – REGISTERED: YES X
23. LOCAL S. S. BOARD NUMBER:
24. COUNTY AND STATE: DADE COUNTY FLORIDA
25. HOME ADDRESS AT TIME OF ENTRY ON ACTIVE DUTY: SEE 9
26. DATE OF ENTRY ON ACTIVE DUTY: 5 DECEMBER 1943
27. MILITARY OCCUPATIONAL SPECIALTY AND NO.: COMMANDING OFFICER, DETACHMENT OF PATIENTS - [illegible]
28. BATTLES AND CAMPAIGNS: EUROPEAN THEATER OF OPERATIONS - AIR OFFENSIVE OVER EUROPE, NORMANDY, NORTHERN FRANCE
29. DECORATIONS AND CITATIONS: EUROPEAN AFRICAN MIDDLE EASTERN THEATER CAMPAIGN RIBBON - DISTINGUISHED FLYING CROSS - AIR MEDAL WITH THREE OAK LEAF CLUSTERS
30. WOUNDS RECEIVED IN ACTION: NONE
31. SERVICE SCHOOLS ATTENDED: PRE FLIGHT SCHOOL, MAXWELL FIELD, ALABAMA; ADVANCED FLYING, FREEMAN FIELD, INDIANA
32. SERVICE OUTSIDE CONTINENTAL U. S. AND RETURN

DATE OF DEPARTURE	DESTINATION	DATE OF ARRIVAL
9 APR 44	EUROPEAN THEATER	12 APR 44
3 OCT 44	U S A	[illegible] OCT 44

33. REASON AND AUTHORITY FOR SEPARATION: WD CIR 485 1944 SR 1-5 - DEMOBILIZATION
34. CURRENT TOUR OF ACTIVE DUTY

Continental Service Years	Months	Days	Foreign Service Years	Months	Days
1	0	6	0	6	9

35. EDUCATION (years): GRAMMAR SCHOOL 8; HIGH SCHOOL 4; COLLEGE 2

INSURANCE NOTICE

IMPORTANT IF PREMIUM IS NOT PAID WHEN DUE OR WITHIN THIRTY-ONE DAYS THEREAFTER, INSURANCE WILL LAPSE. MAKE CHECKS OR MONEY ORDERS PAYABLE TO THE TREASURER OF THE U. S. AND FORWARD TO COLLECTIONS SUBDIVISION, VETERANS ADMINISTRATION, WASHINGTON 25, D. C.

36. Kind of Insurance	37. How Paid	38. Effective Date of Allotment Discontinuance	39. Date of Next Premium Due	40. Premium Due Each Month	41. Intention of Veteran To
Nat. Serv. X	Allotment X	31 MAY 45	30 JUNE 45	6.60	Continue X

42. RIGHT THUMB PRINT

43. REMARKS (This space for completion of above items or entry of other items specified in W. D. Directives): LAPEL BUTTON ISSUED

44. SIGNATURE OF OFFICER BEING SEPARATED

45. PERSONNEL OFFICER (Type name, grade and organization - signature): LEONARD MEYERS 1ST LT., CAC

WD AGO FORM 53-98 November 1944

This form supersedes all previous editions of WD AGO Forms 53 and 280 for officers entitled to a Certificate of Service, which will not be used after receipt of this revision.

5. VETERANS ADMINISTRATION REGIONAL OFFICE COPY (To: Regional Office responsible for address shown in item 9).

Certification of

Military Service

This certifies that Robert C. Sage
13 099 597

was a member of the Regular Army

from February 7, 1943

to December 4, 1943

Service was terminated by Honorable Discharge

Last Grade, Rank, or Rating Aviation Cadet

Active Service Dates Same as above

Honorable Discharge to Accept a Commission.

Given at St. Louis, Missouri, on June 1, 1993

National Personnel Records Center
(Military Personnel Records)
National Archives and Records Administration

THE ARCHIVIST OF THE UNITED STATES IS THE PHYSICAL CUSTODIAN OF THIS PERSON'S MILITARY RECORD.

(This Certification of Military Service is issued in the absence of a copy of the actual Report of Separation, or its equivalent. This document serves as verification of military service and may be used for any official purpose. Not valid without official seal.)

NA FORM 13038 (REV. 10-89)

Appendix F: Military Medals

Table 1: Military Service of Robert C. Sage Locations and Chronology[1]

1. DALHART, Texas- Combat Crew Training, B-17 (Feb.-Mar. 1944)
2. IN TRANSIT:
    a. KEARNEY, Nebraska- picked up aircraft
    b. BANGOR, Maine- repairs to aircraft
    c. GOOSE BAY, Labrador, Canada
    d. KEFLAVIK, Iceland
    e. NUTTS CORNER, Ireland
    f. BURY ST. EDMUNDS, England
3. THURLEIGH, England - 367th Bomb Squadron, 306th Bomb Group (Apr.-Oct. 1944)
4. GLASGOW, Scotland - Board Queen Elizabeth (several days)
5. CAMP SHANKS, New York (1 day)
6. ATLANTIC CITY, New Jersey (2 weeks)
7. LOUISVILLE, Kentucky- Louisville Army Air Base, Combat Crew Convalescent Detachment (Nov. 1944-Sept. 1945)
8. Commanding Officer Convalescent Detachment; let out on the "Point System"
9. FORT DIX, New Jersey- Separation

[1]This Table was compiled by RCS shortly before his death in 2002.

Biography
E. Helene Sage, Ph.D.

Born in Philadelphia in 1946, Helene started riding horses at the age of two, an activity encouraged by her father, who took up riding while stationed in England during World War II. Horses, whether living, carousel, ceramic, lead, or paper, have always been a part of Helene's life. Her parents purchased Spring Hill Farm, in Berks Co., Pennsylvania, in 1959, and Helene, with her brother Bob, instructed, trained, and showed throughout the Northeast from that location until the late 1960s. Helene and her father, Robert Charles Sage, were consistent winners in Pairs Classes with their horses Tom Dooley and Mr. Jay Jay. A graduate of Moravian Preparatory School and Mount Holyoke College, where she majored in Biochemistry with a minor in Latin, Helene traveled progressively westward until she reached Salt Lake City, and eventually, Seattle. While earning a Ph.D. in Biological Sciences at the University of Utah, Helene established a hunter-oriented stable in Draper, Utah, where horses Elko and Crystal Bay enabled her to travel to shows throughout the Intermountain West and California. She also established a stable at White Sands Missile Range (New Mexico) and rode as a stand-in for Paramount Studios in the Western "Bonanza".

A productive career in cell and molecular biology at the University of Washington created a major hiatus in Helene's riding, but the discoveries, travels, and excitement of doing science more than compensated for the departure from things equine. Her science career in Washington ended in 2007 as Member and Chair of the Hope Heart Program at the Seattle-based Benaroya Research Institute at Virginia Mason. Helene's collection of antique carousel horses, Western Americana, and Native American horse gear now resides in the home she shares with her husband, Paul Bornstein, M.D., near Santa Fe, New Mexico.

An author of over 300 published scientific articles and Western-related commentaries and catalogs, Helene's new book, *Bridle Rosettes: Two Centuries of Equine Adornment*, has recently been published by Schiffer Publishing, Ltd. In fulfillment of a lifelong dream, Helene's father also moved West, to ranching country in Montana. Upon his death his World War II diary, kept under wraps for 60 years, and related photographs were given to his daughter, with the unstated wish to share in some way his experience of those earlier days with Americans of later generations. *The Clay Pigeons* was written to honor that aspiration.

Monty (Montana Sky), a registered Thoroughbred, and Helene Sage, at Las Campanas Equestrian Center, Santa Fe, New Mexico, 2010. Photograph by Paul Bornstein.

Bibliography

Brokaw, Tom. *The Greatest Generation.* New York, New York: Random House, 1998.

Ehli, Nick, editor. *Faces of Freedom – Gallatin Valley Remembers World War II.* Bozeman, Montana: The Bozeman Daily Chronicle, a division of Pioneer Newspapers, Inc., Rick Weaver, publisher, 2002.

Egan, Timothy. *The Long Darkness – Surviving the Great American Dust Bowl.* Gloucestershire, U.K.: Tempus Publishing, Ltd., 2006.

Richardson, Allan B., Bairnsfather, John A., Haberman, Philip W., Owen, Shubel J., Murtha, Edward T., and Leatherman, William A., *Squadron Diary, 367th Bombardment Squadron (H), 1942-45*, compiled & edited by Russell A. Strong. Charlotte, North Carolina: 306th Bomb Group Historical Association, March, 1993.

Strong, Russell A., *First Over Germany- A History of the 306th Bombardment Group.* Charlotte, North Carolina: Russell Strong, 1990.

Strong, Russell A., ed., *306th Bomb Group Association Directory.* Charlotte, North Carolina: 306th Bomb Group Association, September 15, 2002.

Strong, Russell A., *Combat Crews-The 306th Bombardment Group (H), 1942-1945.* Charlotte, North Carolina: 306th Bomb Group Association, September, 2004.

Westgate, Charles J., Major, USAF. *The Reich Wreckers: An Analysis of the 306th Bomb Group During World War II.* Air Command and Staff College, Air University, Maxwell AFB, Alabama, 1998. (Graduate Thesis, Internet Access, December, 2010).

Boeing B-17 Flying Fortress, Wikipedia (http://en.wikipedia.org/wiki/B-17_Flying_Fortress). November 15, 2010

Watson, Emmett. "Therc's Still One B-17 in Seattle, Waiting for Us." *306th Echoes*, October, 1992.

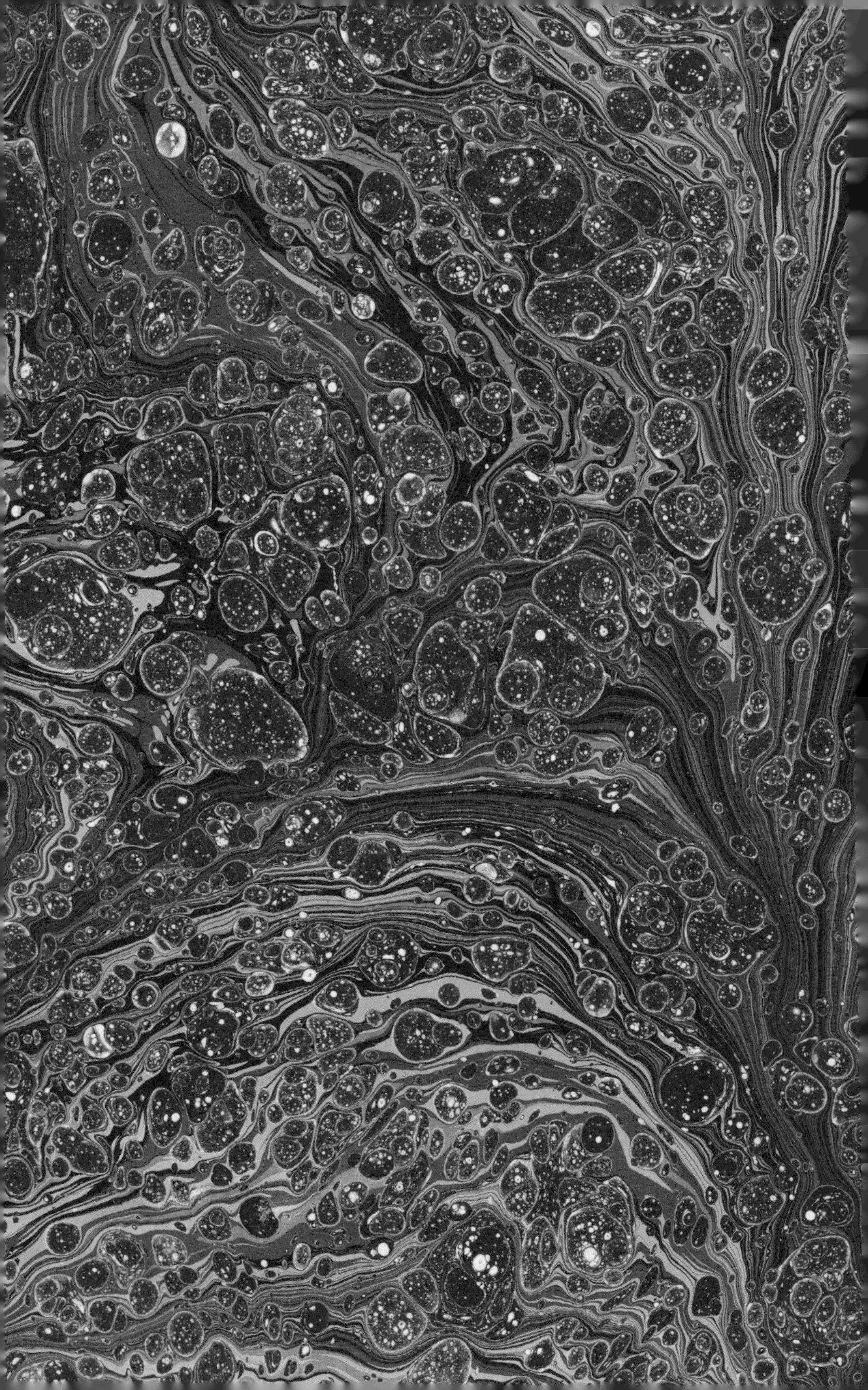